SPECIAL THINGS FOR SPECIAL DAYS

OTHER GOOD YEAR® BOOKS IN LANGUAGE ARTS & READING

DO YOU READ ME?   *Practical Approaches to Teaching Reading Comprehension*
Arnold A. Griese

I CAN MAKE IT ON MY OWN   *Functional Reading Ideas and Activities for Daily Survival*
Michelle Berman and Linda Shevitz

GALAXY OF GAMES   *For Reinforcing Writing Skills*
Jerry Mallett

IMAGINE THAT!   *Illustrated Poems and Creative Learning Experiences*
Joyce King and Carol Katzman

LANGUAGE ARTS IDEA BOOK   *Classroom Activities for Children*
Joanne Schaff

MAINSTREAMING LANGUAGE ARTS AND SOCIAL STUDIES   *Special Ideas and Activities for the Whole Class*
Anne H. Adams, Charles R. Coble, Paul B. Hounshell

NEW DIMENSIONS IN ENGLISH   *An Idea Book of Language Arts Activities for Middle and Secondary School Teachers*
Joanne Schaff

OUNCE OF PREVENTION PLUS A POUND OF CURE   *Tests and Techniques for Aiding Individual Readers*
Ronald W. Bruton

PHORGAN'S PHONICS
Harry W. Forgan

READING CORNER   *Ideas, Games, and Activities for Individualizing Reading*
Harry W. Forgan

READING FOR SURVIVAL IN TODAY'S SOCIETY   *Volumes I and II*
Anne H. Adams, Anne Flowers, Elsa E. Woods

SUCCESS IN READING AND WRITING SERIES
Anne H. Adams, Elizabeth Bebensee, Helen Cappleman, Judith Connors, Mary Johnson

TOTALACTION   *Ideas and Activities for Teaching Children Ages Five to Eight*
Pat Short and Billee Davidson

WRITING UP A STORM   *Creative Writing Ideas and Activities for the Middle Grades*
Linda Polon and Aileen Cantwell

WRITING CORNER
Arnold Cheyney

For information about these or other Good Year ® books in Science, Math, Social Studies, General Methods, and Centers, write to

Good Year Books
Scott, Foresman and Company
1900 E. Lake Avenue
Glenview, Illinois 60025

SPECIAL THINGS FOR SPECIAL DAYS

Holiday Ideas and Activities for Teaching Children Ages Five to Eight

Pat Short
Billee Davidson

Scott, Foresman and Company
Glenview, Illinois
Dallas, TX
Oakland, NJ
Palo Alto, CA
Tucker, GA
London, England

6 7 8 9 10-MAL-88 87 86 85 84 83 82

to those special people who have
shared the joys of learning

CONTENTS

INTRODUCTION

This is a resource book of ideas and activities for teachers to use to further the basic skills of children aged five to eight by capitalizing on their natural interest in Halloween, Thanksgiving, Christmas, Valentine's Day, and Easter.

Some activities are adaptations of familiar favorites and some are totally new. All subject areas are included, and the ability levels accommodate children from kindergarten through grade three. The activities can be used successfully as described, or they can be modified to suit your own personal interests and the abilities of the children within your class. All materials in SPECIAL THINGS FOR SPECIAL DAYS —whether Workcard Sets or Handwork—may be presented to an entire class, to a group of children, or to an individual child, depending upon your own classroom organization. The activities for any "Special Day" can easily be altered to suit any other— simply change a picture, alter a phrase, or reword a caption.

We hope particularly that the hints included for you, the primary teacher, will be helpful in making every day more enjoyable for you and, indeed, special for your students.

SKILLS
The following skills are at the core of the thematic units in this book. By capitalizing on the children's natural interest in SPECIAL DAYS and their enjoyment of SPECIAL THINGS you can enrich your program while improving the basic skills of the children in your classroom.

development of communication skills

development of recall skills

development of visual discrimination

expansion of interpretative skills

extension of vocabulary

growth in the ability to be cooperative and understanding

growth of fine motor skills

reinforcement of basic language skills

reinforcement of basic number facts and operations

reinforcement of phonetic sounds

SPECIAL
THINGS
FOR
SPECIAL
DAYS

HALLOWEEN

WORKCARD SETS

Story Starters
Pumpkin Patch

BOOKLETS

GAMES AND ACTIVITIES

The Witch's Hat
Haunted House
Safe at Home
Hallo-Sounds
Story Illustration
Halloween Night
Things to Do With a Pumpkin
    (or Several Pumpkins)

HANDWORK

Straw Skeleton
Glue Pictures
Pumpkin Vines
Jumping Jacks
Perching Pumpkin
Ghost
Folded Bats
Halloween Whoo-s

DRAMATICS AND PHYSICAL ACTIVITIES

Mood-ments
Team o'Lantern

WORKSHEETS

Whoo-oo Are You?
Boo!
Fill-Ins
Cut-Outs
Symmetry
Pumpkin Face
Halloween Mask
A Ghostly Tale
Oo-ooh, ooh
Crackling Clues

BOOK LIST

WORKCARD SETS

Story Starters

These starters will encourage some scary and exciting stories, whether used individually or as a group speaking and writing experience.

> As I crept up the stairs of the gloomy old house, I heard . . .

> The door creaked shut. They were locked in!

> A frightening yowl startled Richie . . .

> Ooh! It's dark in here . . .

> A horrible ghostly shape drifted towards me and then . . .

> All of a sudden the lights went out!

> The moon, shining through the trees, made a path which led me to . . .

> The old witch cackled and . . .

> From behind a gnarled tree sprang . . .

> I noticed the green eyes and smirking smile and then . . .

The children will also enjoy creating and recording sounds to enhance the stories as they are read to the class.

Individual chalkboards are an aid in any story-writing assignments. Children may draft out their stories on the chalkboards and gain assistance from you without the handicap of having work crossed out or erased. Completed stories can be copied onto paper or in books, giving the children extra practice in handwriting and copying. Small, portable chalkboards are terrific, too, for quick arithmetic drills.

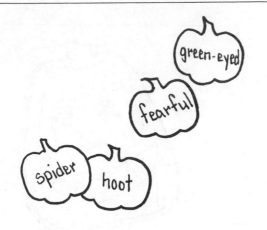

Pumpkin Patch

The workcards for this creative writing or story telling activity are pumpkin shapes in green, yellow, orange, and black paper. These shapes can be placed:

on a chart made to resemble a pumpkin patch

inside hollowed-out pumpkins

inside small, plastic pumpkins

in Halloween paper cups

in child-decorated tin cans

The child chooses one Halloween word from each category:

creatures: ghost, goblin, witch, wizard, jack-o-lantern, skeleton, cat, owl, bat, devil, spider, toad, demon

feelings: happy, excited, scared, fearful, nervous, shaky, anxious, shivering

sounds: swish, creak, boo, hiss, yeowl, meow, crash, cackle, bubble, hoot, whine, groan, cry, moan, wail, shout, yell

descriptions: ugly, wrinkled, bony, green-eyed, gnarled, scary, grinning, smirking, treacherous, dangerous, magically, shadowy, murky, gloomy, mysterious, misty, haunted

The child then uses the four words in the opening sentence of his written or oral story.

For example, using ''wizard,'' ''fearful,'' ''moan,'' and ''gnarled,'' a child might form a sentence such as, ''The gnarled, old wizard gave a fearful moan.''

Young children, perhaps, may only be asked to choose a card from the categories of creatures and descriptions, or to create a single sentence rather than an entire paragraph or story.

BOOKLETS

The magic that surrounds Halloween can lead to exciting booklets containing imaginative descriptions and bold pictures.

The children can work on individual booklets or they can share their ideas while making a group booklet.

Some titles for Halloween booklets are:

Goblins, Ghouls, and Ghosts

On Halloween Night . . .

Costumes

Halloween Safety

Boo!

Black and Orange

Sights and Frights

Jack-o-Lanterns

Halloween Handouts

The Witch's Brew

Activities and assignments of all types are greatly enhanced by student photography. Even young children can successfully operate the modern, easy-to-handle slide, photograph, and movie cameras. Displays and presentations can be made on any topic. The children can write their own captions and commentaries.

GAMES AND ACTIVITIES

The Witch's Hat

The children sit in a circle while the witch sits in the middle and hides his or her eyes.

The children pass around a paper witch's hat as they recite the following verse:

> *In the night full of dark and gloom*
> *The witch is riding on her broom*
> *And she is cackling to her cat*
> *"I'm going to search till I find my hat."*

When the verse ends, the child holding the hat keeps it, and *all* of the children put their hands behind their backs.

The witch keeps both eyes hidden until he or she is given permission to guess who is holding the hat.

The witch has three guesses and if successful may have another turn.

If the witch does not guess correctly, the child with the hat goes in the middle to be the witch.

The verse used in this game may be adapted to accommodate boys by changing the character to a wizard.

Older children may enjoy learning an extended version of the Halloween verse:

> *In the night full of dark and gloom*
> *The witch is riding on her broom*
> *And she is cackling to her cat*
> *"I'm going to search till I find my hat."*
> *She swoops by the great gnarled tree*
> *And asks the hoot owl if he did see*
> *Any ghosts or goblins with a pointed hat*
> *That was old and wrinkled and black as a bat.*
> *"I have to find my hat, and soon*
> *For without it I'm afraid of the moon!"*

Haunted House

Two players take alternating turns.

One player chooses an answer card and places it in a window that follows an equal sign.

The other player then quickly completes the equation orally; if the equation is correct, he or she keeps the answer card. If the equation is incorrect, the first player receives the answer card.

At the end of the game, the winner is the player with the most answer cards.

Children can print directly on laminated gameboards with dark-colored crayons. After the game, the surface is wiped clean using paper toweling. If you prefer, staple several small pieces of newsprint over the window panes or answer spaces. Children can then tear off and discard the used pieces.

Either of these methods can also be employed on phonics and arithmetic workcards, in order to give the children a change from printing or drawing their answers in notebooks. It makes marking easier, too.

Safe at Home

Two to four players may participate.

One dice (a wooden cube which has been numbered one through three), markers, and the gameboard are necessary.

The players each roll the dice and move accordingly.

They must also follow any special instructions given on the gameboard.

The first player to reach home safely is the winner.

Hallo-Sounds

The teacher uses Halloween words and characters to reinforce phonetic sounds.

The teacher may choose a word such as pumpkin, witch, cat, goblin, skeleton, spider, ghost, or toad depending on which sound requires practice.

The activity for the short "u" in pumpkin might be the following:

> The teacher draws several pumpkins on a chalkboard or on a large piece of paper and prints a short "u" word on each one. If a child can read the word on the pumpkin, he or she may draw in the pumpkin's face.

Great care need not be taken with the drawings for this activity since they will probably not be reusable.

Story Illustration

The following Halloween story is designed to develop the children's awareness of details and interpretive skills.

The story may be printed on a large chart, recorded on a tape, or read to the children.

Either working individually, or in very small groups, the children may illustrate the story and give it a title.

It was October thirty-first, and Jeffrey was having a Halloween party. He had invited some friends and had helped his mother to decorate the living room.

They had hung orange and black streamers around the room. Jeffrey carved a jack-o'-lantern with a smirking mouth and wide eyes. He placed a paper skeleton in the corner above a lamp. The lamp shone on the green-eyed skeleton making it look very spooky, indeed! Mother had baked a special Halloween cake and it was on the table near the tub that Jeffrey had ready for apple bobbing.

Some children had arrived. There was a girl dressed all in black with a long tail, two little pointed ears, and even some long, black whiskers. A small child had on a white sheet and shouted "Boo!" at everyone. One tall boy had a long, black cape that he swirled around himself. Jeffrey looked funny with a large, red nose, shaggy, orange hair, and two large shoes sticking out beneath his baggy, polka-dotted suit.

The doorbell rang and two more children came in. The first child, a boy, was in a silver-colored outfit with large antennae and a flashing light. The little girl carried a basket of treats and wore a red, hooded cape.

Just then Mother carried in the pumpkin-shaped cake. The Halloween party was ready to begin.

Halloween Night

The children sit in a large circle and take turns completing the sentence "As I was walking on Halloween night I saw . . ."

Each child must recite the preceding sentence, naming something that could be seen on Halloween night.

The children should be encouraged to use as many descriptive adjectives as possible in order to extend their vocabularies.

In any game or activity where the teacher feels competition is needed to promote interest, "tokens" can be used as rewards. A number of articles may serve as tokens; including poker chips, buttons, simply cut paper shapes, squares of colored paper, or tickets torn from a purchased roll.

Things to Do With a Pumpkin (or Several Pumpkins)

Describe it.

Measure it.

Weigh it.

Compare its size or weight to other pumpkins or other articles.

Have a jack-o'-lantern designing contest.

Carve it and empty it.

Count the seeds.

Roast and eat the seeds.

String the seeds.

Make seed pictures.

Plant the seeds.

> They may be planted in foil trays, paper cups, plastic pots, or garden pots.
>
> Seeds will grow in a variety of mediums, such as soil, sand, water, or vermiculite.
>
> Allow the seeds to germinate with or without sunlight.
>
> Record or graph what happens.

Stew the pulp.

> Note the changes.
>
> Bake pumpkin bread, cake, or pie.

Note the effects of time and air on the jack-o'-lantern.

Write stories and poems pretending to be:

> in a pumpkin patch
>
> a pumpkin just bought by some children
>
> a discarded jack-o'-lantern

HANDWORK

Straw Skeleton

Each child needs a piece of black construction paper, white drinking straws, and scraps of white paper.

The straws should be cut in different lengths so that they resemble the various bones in a skeleton.

The straw skeleton must be laid out on the paper. When the desired form is attained, the straws are glued down one at a time.

A head in the form of a skull is cut from the white scraps.

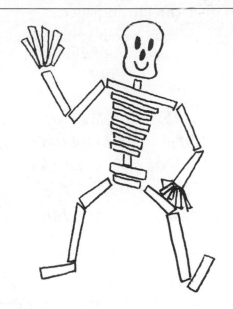

Glue Pictures

Squeeze white, bondfast glue in a ghostly shape on a long, narrow piece of tagboard.

Older children could be encouraged to make several overlapping ghosts.

Let glue dry overnight.

When glue is thoroughly dry, brush a dark blue or black wash over the entire surface.

For a shiny effect, brush on a coat of shellac.

Pumpkin Vines

To make the vines, each child needs a piece of shiny-surfaced white paper, a drinking straw, and orange construction paper. (A short piece of a drinking straw is easier for the child to handle.)

The child drops a small amount of black paint onto the shiny-surfaced paper and spreads the paint around by blowing through the straw.

Children should be reminded that their straws are not to touch the paper. (Added drops of paint may be needed so that the blown vines of paint will extend over the entire paper.)

Pumpkins may be cut from orange construction paper and glued onto the vine.

What do you do with all those wet paintings? Some alternatives are to hang the paintings on skirt racks, clip them to wires or cords with clothespins, pin them to a tackboard, or lay them over a drying rack.

Jumping Jacks

A pumpkin shape is cut from a fairly large piece of orange construction paper.

Long, wide paper strips are cut from black, green, orange, or yellow construction paper; accordion or spring folded; and attached to the pumpkin shape to form arms and legs.

Each child then traces and cuts out his or her own hands and feet from black, green, orange, or yellow construction paper and attaches them to the pumpkin.

Hair and facial features are cut out and pasted to the pumpkin.

Hats, glasses, earrings, and other details may be added, if desired.

The Jumping Jacks may be suspended with string or thread.

Perching Pumpkin

Each child traces and cuts out eight circles from orange construction paper. The paper should be at least 6'' (15 cm) in diameter.

Each circle is folded in half and a small amount of glue is applied to one-half of the back side.

This glued semi-circle is then attached to the back half of another folded circle.

This process is continued until all of the folded circles are glued together and the top view resembles the illustration.

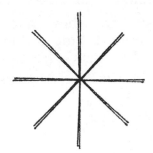

Arms and legs are made from accordion-folded paper strips and are glued to the body.

Hands and feet may be attached.

A gentleman's hat may be made from construction paper by attaching a cylindrical crown to a circular brim.

The hat is glued to the top of the pumpkin.

Facial features may be made from scraps and attached by folding back small tabs on which to put the glue.

When finished, the children may choose suitable places to perch their pumpkins.

Ghost

Each child places one hand on a piece of white paper so that the little finger and the thumb are widely spaced from the other three fingers.

The child traces around his or her hand, extending the lines down to the wrist, to make a ghostlike shape.

The ghosts are then cut out and mounted on dark blue or black paper. (For a spooky effect, the ghosts could be attached to the background with paper springs.)

Scraps of black paper or a black crayon can be used to make eyes.

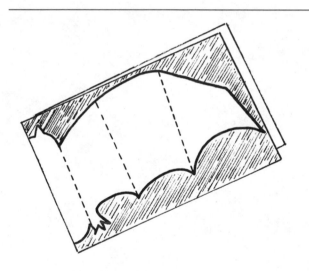

Folded Bats

On a folded piece of black construction paper the child draws a simple bat.

The shaded portions are cut away and the paper is folded along the dotted lines.

A hole is punched in the body section so the bat can be suspended.

Halloween Whoo-s

Shapes of various sizes can be torn or cut from Halloween-colored construction paper and glued together to make Halloween Whoo-s.

Supply the children with shopping bags, scraps of paper, scissors, glue, and staples and using some imagination they can create trick or treat bags for Halloween night. The decorated bags are also handy for taking home handwork or party goodies from school. Children will have fun designing shopping bags for any special occasion.

DRAMATICS AND PHYSICAL ACTIVITIES

Mood-ments

Creative movements, drama, and pantomime are easily encouraged during the excitement of Halloween.

Ask the children to move, react, and pantomime the rhythms, words, and moods of:

> Halloween songs
>
> recorded sounds of owls, cats, squeaking doors, shouts, and moans
>
> loud, eery, or frightening music
>
> Halloween poetry

Give instructions to move like a:

> creeping cat
>
> flickering candle
>
> bubbling cauldron
>
> swooping bat
>
> wobbly skeleton
>
> floating ghost
>
> frightened boy
>
> creaking door
>
> cackling witch
>
> gnarled wizard
>
> pouncing cat
>
> wailing goblin
>
> treacherous sorcerer
>
> hooting owl
>
> grinning jack-o'-lantern

Pair the children for shadow movements in which one child is the actor and the other is the shadow.

Movement and drama activities should rely on the stimulation of imagination and spontaneous reactions. Verbal directions, stories, music, poems, lighting, and simple props can all be used to suggest who, what, when, where, and how. To maximize the value and the results of the activities it is beneficial to include the following steps: stimulation, imagination, improvisation, discussion, reaction, and performance.

Team-o'-Lanterns

This is a relay game in which the children are divided into even teams.

The team members stand in a line, facing a pumpkin that has been drawn either on a chalkboard or on a large piece of paper that is affixed to the wall.

The first team member holds a piece of chalk or a dark-colored crayon, runs up to his or her team's pumpkin, draws one facial feature, runs back to the team, passes the chalk or crayon to the second team member, and then goes to the end of the team's line.

When the second team member has the chalk or crayon, the same steps are followed.

When the last team member has finished, he or she goes to the end of the team's line and the team members sit down.

The winning team is the first to have all of its members sitting down.

For variation team members could be instructed to hop, skip, crabwalk, bunnyhop, bounce a ball, balance a bean bag, or complete a combination of these actions.

WORKSHEETS

Page 20
Whoo-oo Are You! The equations are completed and the dots joined consecutively according to the answers.

Page 21
Boo! The children count by fives to join the dots and find this ghostly creature.

Pages 22, 23
Fill-Ins Arithmetic equations or phonetic words to be completed, sight words to be read, or color words to be colored should be printed in the hats and pumpkins before these worksheets are duplicated.

To accommodate the skills needing practice and the varying abilities of the children in your class, perhaps you'd prefer to make several masters and print different skill tasks on each one.

Page 24
Cut-Outs The equations are answered and corrected. The figures are then colored, cut out, and glued on a separate sheet of paper to form the basis for a Halloween picture. Other details can be added to the picture and a story may be written or told about it.

Page 25
Symmetry The other half of the jack-o'-lantern is drawn by the child. It can then be colored.

Page 26
Pumpkin Face Using a pencil, the child traces over all of the dotted lines. The paper is cut on the double lines and the facial features are cut out and pasted on to turn this pumpkin into a jack-o'-lantern. It can then be colored when the glue or paste is dry.

Page 27

Halloween Mask The children draw themselves as they would like to look on Halloween, or create a character and its costume. In either case, a story may be written or told about the finished picture.

Page 28

A Ghostly Tale This can be run onto lined paper, a story written, and the ghostly shape cut out and displayed.

Page 29

Oo-ooh, ooh The picture is completed, colored, and a story is told or written.

Pages 30, 31, 32, 33

Crackling Clues The children should decode the puzzles and print the answers. They may complete only one puzzle, or the entire set of puzzles may be stapled together with a cover to form a booklet. The solutions for these puzzles are:

1.   Boo
    oRange
  moOn
     Owl
   puMpkin

2.   Poison
    bUbbles
    sMirk
  pumPkin
    sKeleton
   shIvering
   gNarled

3. blackCat
    shAky
   shoUts
   HalLoween
   canDy
    bRoom
    mOon
  gobliN

4.   uGly
    Hoot
  OctOber
   hisS
  frighTened

5.   Broom
  skuLl
   afrAid
   caCkle
   creaKy
  magiCian
    bAt
   cosTume

6.   Wobbly
   wItch
 haunTed
   sCared
   wHines

7.   maSk
  pumPkins
   hIss
   shaDow
 frightEned
   daRk

8.   Spider
  masK
   dEvil
   gobLin
 excitEd
   wiTch
    Owl
 hauNt

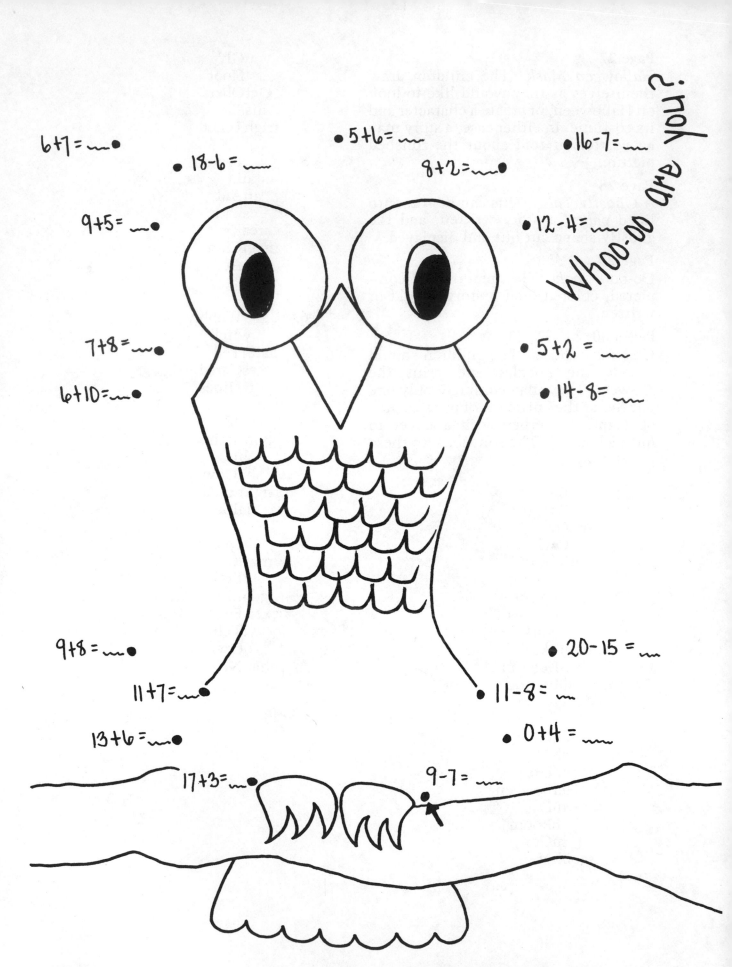

6+7 = ﹏•

18-6 = ﹏

5+6 = ﹏

8+2 = ﹏

16-7 = ﹏

Whoo-oo are you?

9+5 = ﹏•

12-4 = ﹏

7+8 = ﹏•

6+10 = ﹏•

5+2 = ﹏

14-8 = ﹏

9+8 = ﹏•

20-15 = ﹏

11+7 = ﹏•

11-8 = ﹏

13+6 = ﹏•

0+4 = ﹏

17+3 = ﹏•

9-7 = ﹏

20

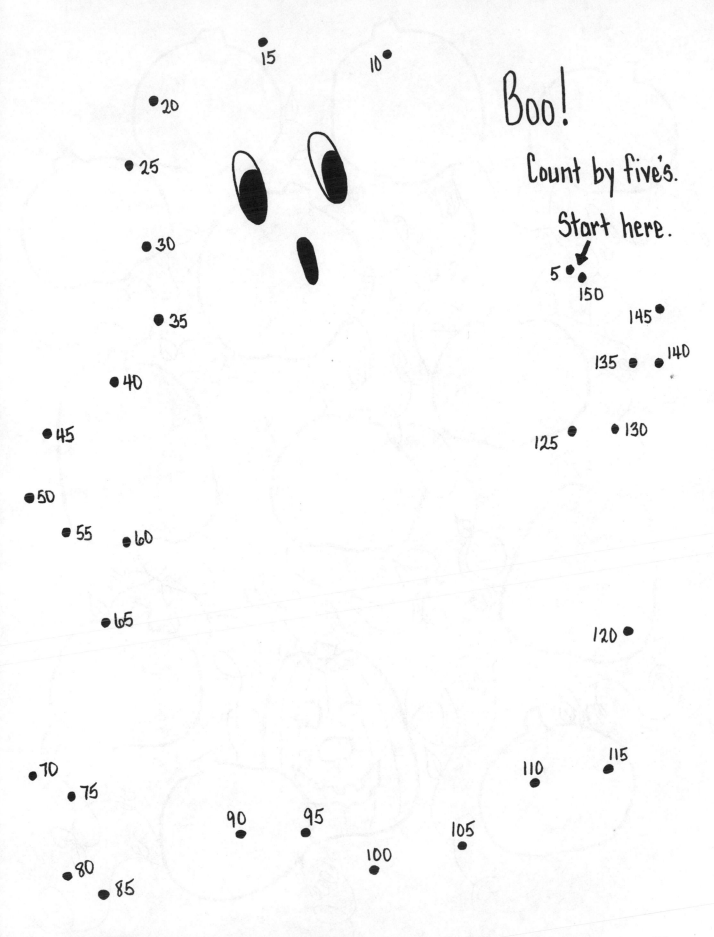

Boo!

Count by five's.

Start here.

From *Special Things for Special Days* © 1980 by Goodyear Publishing Company, Inc.

21

22

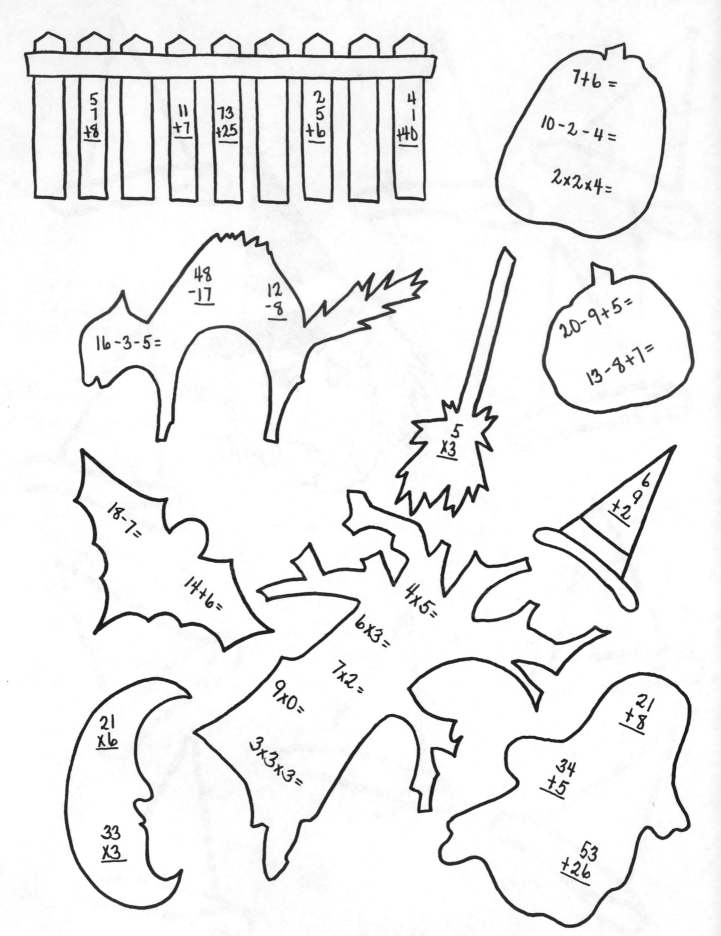

$$\begin{array}{r} 5 \\ 1 \\ +8 \\ \hline \end{array}$$

$$\begin{array}{r} 11 \\ +7 \\ \hline \end{array}$$

$$\begin{array}{r} 73 \\ +25 \\ \hline \end{array}$$

$$\begin{array}{r} 2 \\ 5 \\ +6 \\ \hline \end{array}$$

$$\begin{array}{r} 4 \\ 1 \\ +40 \\ \hline \end{array}$$

$7+6 =$

$10-2-4 =$

$2 \times 2 \times 4 =$

$$\begin{array}{r} 48 \\ -17 \\ \hline \end{array}$$

$$\begin{array}{r} 12 \\ -8 \\ \hline \end{array}$$

$16-3-5 =$

$20-9+5 =$

$13-8+7 =$

$$\begin{array}{r} 5 \\ \times 3 \\ \hline \end{array}$$

$$\begin{array}{r} 9 \ 6 \\ +2 \\ \hline \end{array}$$

$18-7 =$

$14+6 =$

$4 \times 5 =$

$6 \times 3 =$

$7 \times 2 =$

$9 \times 0 =$

$3 \times 3 \times 3 =$

$$\begin{array}{r} 21 \\ \times 6 \\ \hline \end{array}$$

$$\begin{array}{r} 33 \\ \times 3 \\ \hline \end{array}$$

$$\begin{array}{r} 21 \\ +8 \\ \hline \end{array}$$

$$\begin{array}{r} 34 \\ +5 \\ \hline \end{array}$$

$$\begin{array}{r} 53 \\ +26 \\ \hline \end{array}$$

24

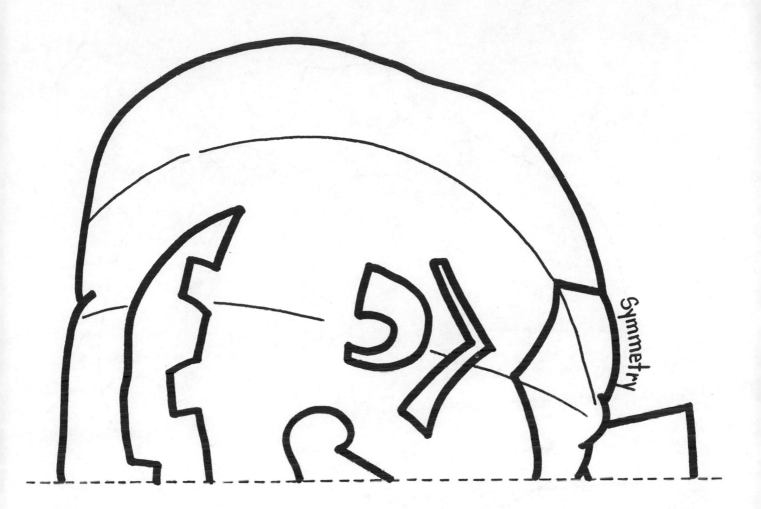

Symmetry

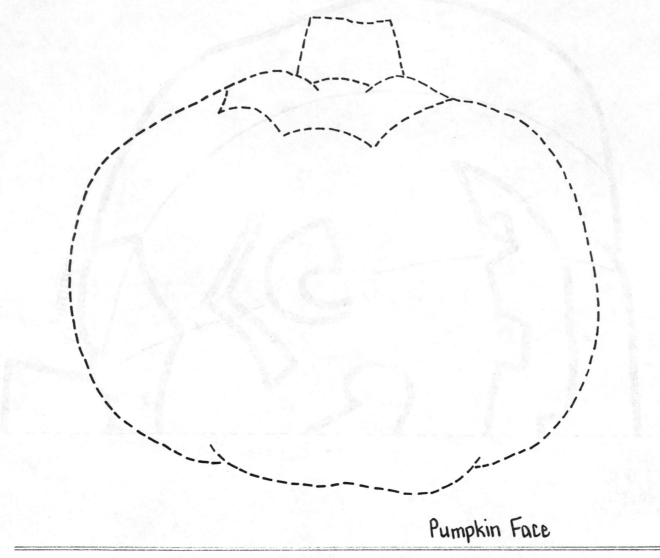

Pumpkin Face

A Ghostly Tale   by

Oo-ooh, ooh

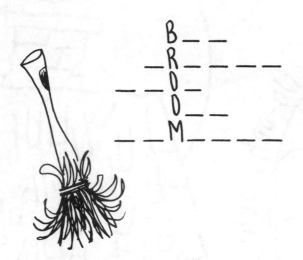

B _ _ _   what a ghost might say
_ R _ _ _ _   a Halloween color
_ _ O _ _   the only light in the woods
_ _ O _ _   a very wise bird
_ _ M _ _ _ _   this grows on a vine

Crackling Clues — Puzzle One

P _ _ _ _ _ _   a bottle with skull and crossbones
_ U _ _ _ _ _   the witch's cauldron...
_ _ M _ _ _   a sneaky grin
_ _ _ P _ _ _   a vegetable that makes a pie
_ _ K _ _ _ _ _   skull and bones
_ _ I _ _ _ _ _   shaking from fright or cold
_ N _ _ _ _ _   badly twisted

Crackling Clues — Puzzle Two

30

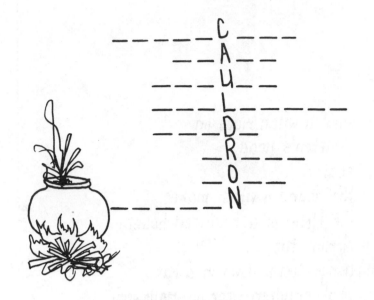

```
_ _ _ _ _ C _ _ _
  _ _ A _ _ _
  _ _ U _ _
  _ _ _ L _ _ _
  _ _ D _ _ _
  _ R _ _ _
_ _ _ _ _ N
```

a witch's pet
unsteady
loud calls
a special day
a Halloween treat
carries a witch
a big yellow...
a ghost's friend

```
_ G _ _
_ H _ _ _
_ _ O _ _ _
_ _ _ S _
_ _ _ _ _ T _ _ _ _
```

the witch's face
...says the owl
the month of Halloween
an angry cat says...
scared

B _ _ _ _ _ _   what a witch rides on
_ _ _ _ L _ _   skeleton's head
_ _ _ A _ _ _   scared
_ _ _ C _ _ _   the sound a witch makes
_ _ _ K _ _   the floor of a haunted house
_ _ C _ _ _   Merlin, the . . .
_ _ A _ _   hangs upside down in a cave
_ _ _ T _ _ _ _   what children wear on Halloween

Crackling Clues ——— Puzzle Five

W _ _ _ _ _ _   shaky
_ I _ _ _   stirs the bubbling cauldron
_ _ T _ _ _   a . . . house
_ C _ _ _   frightened
_ H _ _ _   a lonely dog . . .

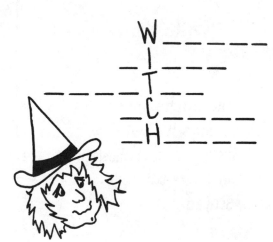

Crackling Clues ——— Puzzle Six

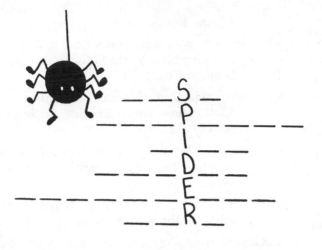

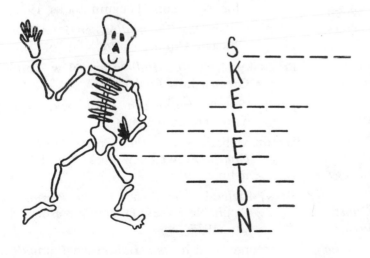

Puzzle Seven

_ _ S _ _   it hides your face
_ _ _ P _ _ _ _ _   children carve these
_ _ _ I _ _ _   a cat says this
_ _ _ D _ _ _   the moon casts a ...
_ _ _ _ E _ _ _   afraid
_ _ R _   it is ... dark at night

Crackling Clues

Puzzle Eight

S _ _ _ _ _ _   has eight legs
_ _ K _ _ _ _   worn on Halloween
_ _ E _ _ _ _   has horns and a pointed tail
_ _ _ L _ _ _   ghost's friend
_ _ _ _ E _ _   how children feel on Halloween
_ _ T _ _   rides on a broom
_ _ O _   can see better at night
_ _ _ N _   ghosts ... houses

Crackling Clues

BOOK LIST

Alexander, Sue. *More Witch, Goblin and Ghost Stories.* New York: Pantheon Books, 1978.

Anderson, Lonzo. *The Halloween Party.* New York: Charles Scribner's Sons, 1974.

Balian, Lorna. *Humbug Witch.* Nashville: Abingdon Press, 1965.

Barth, Edna. *Jack-o'-Lantern.* New York: Seabury Press, 1974.

Barton, Byron. *Hester.* New York: Greenwillow Books, 1975.

Calhoun, Mary. *The Witch of Hissing Hill.* New York: William Morrow and Co., 1964.

Carley, Wayne. *The Witch Who Forgot.* Toronto, Ontario: Thomas Nelson and Sons, 1975.

Carrick, Carol. *Old Mother Witch.* New York: Seabury Press, 1975.

Coombs, Patricia. *Dorrie and the Halloween Plot.* New York: Lothrop, Lee, and Shepard, 1976.

Cooper, Paulette. *Let's Find Out About Halloween.* New York: Franklin Watts, 1972.

Degan, Bruce. *Aunt Possum and the Pumpkin Man.* New York: Harper and Row, 1977.

Devlin, Wende and Harry. *Old Black Witch.* New York: Parent's Magazine Press, 1966.

Devlin, Wende and Harry. *Old Witch Rescues Halloween.* New York: Parent's Magazine Press, 1972.

Dobrin, Arnold. *Make a Witch, Make a Goblin.* New York: Four Winds Press, 1977.

Edmondson, Madeleine. *The Witch's Egg.* New York: Seabury Press, 1974.

Gezi, Kal. *The Mystery of the Live Ghosts.* Elgin, Illinois: Child's World, 1978.

Gibbons, Gail. *Things to Make and Do for Halloween.* New York: Franklin Watts, 1976.

Glovach, Linda. *The Little Witch's Black Magic Cookbook.* Englewood Cliffs, New Jersey: Prentice-Hall, 1972.

Glovach, Linda. *Little Witch's Halloween Book.* Englewood Cliffs, New Jersey: Prentice-Hall, 1975.

Keats, Ezra-Jack. *The Trip.* New York: Greenwillow Books, 1979.

Johnson, Hannah Lyons. *From Seed to Jack-o'-Lantern.* New York: Lothrop, Lee, and Shepard Co., 1974.

Kahl, Virginia. *Gunhilde and the Halloween Spell.* New York: Charles Scribner's Sons, 1975.

Low, Alice. *The Witch Who Was Afraid of Witches.* New York: Pantheon Books, 1978.

McCaffery, Janet. *The Swamp Witch.* New York: William Morrow and Co., 1970.

McGovern, Ann. *Squeaks, and Squiggles, and Ghostly Giggles.* New York: Four Winds Press, 1973.

Martin, Patricia Miles. *The Pumpkin Patch.* New York: G. P. Putnam's Sons, 1966.

Moore, Lillian. *See My Lovely Poison Ivy.* New York: Atheneum, 1975.

Mooser, Stephen. *The Ghost with the Halloween Hiccups.* New York: Franklin Watts, 1977.

Nicoll, Helen, and Pienkowski, Jan. *Meg and Mog.* New York: Penguin Books, 1972.

Oldfield, Pamela. *The Halloween Pumpkin.* Chicago: Children's Press, 1976.

Prelutsky, Jack. *It's Halloween.* New York: Greenwillow Books, 1977.

Purdy, Susan. *Halloween Cookbook.* New York: Franklin Watts, 1977.

Schulz, Charles. *It's the Great Pumpkin, Charlie Brown.* New York: World Publishing, 1967.

Shaw, Richard. *The Kitten in the Pumpkin Patch.* New York: Frederick Warne and Co., 1973.

St. George, Judith. *The Halloween Pumpkin Smasher.* New York: G. P. Putnam's Sons, 1978.

Terris, Susan. *The Upstairs Witch and the Downstairs Witch.* New York: Doubleday, 1970

Tudor, Tasha. *Pumpkin Moonshine*. New York: Henry Z. Walck, Inc., 1962.

Wahl, Jan. *Pleasant Fieldmouse's Halloween Party*. New York: G. P. Putnam's Sons, 1974.

Wahl, Jan. *The Muffletumps' Halloween Scare*. Chicago: Follett Publishing Co., 1977.

Wiseman, Bernard. *Halloween with Morris and Borris*. New York: Dodd, Mead, and Co., 1975.

Teacher's Resource Book:

Barth, Edna. *Witches, Pumpkins, and Grinning Ghosts: The Story of the Halloween Symbols*. New York: Seabury Press, 1972.

Thanksgiving

WORKCARD SETS

Turkey Tails
Recipe Cards

BOOKLETS

GAMES AND ACTIVITIES

Collages
The Pilgrims Sailed
Thoughtful Spins
Picto-Story
Sharing
Thanksgiving Luncheon
Recipe Books
Centers or Corners
Tail Feathers

HANDWORK

Turkeys
Murals
Samplers
Trace-a-Friend
Seed Pictures
Folded-Paper Log Cabin
Evergreens

DRAMATICS AND PHYSICAL ACTIVITIES

You Were There
Run, Little Turkeys

WORKSHEETS

Fill-Ins
Maze
A House is a House
Symmetry
Turkey Tracings
A Thanksgiving Feast
Things Harvested in Autumn
Pilgrim Pastimes

BOOK LIST

WORKCARD SETS

Turkey Tails

These feather-shaped workcards are to be pinned or paper-clipped to a cut-out turkey.

The children should choose the workcards individually, or one workcard may be chosen as the assignment for a small group.

The feathers might instruct the children to do the following things:

> Print the menu for Thanksgiving dinner. List the foods in alphabetical order.

> Draw a turkey. Trace your fingers for his tail feathers.

> Think of two words that are synonyms for "thank." Use each one in a sentence.

> Make a booklet about Thanksgiving today or Thanksgiving long ago.

> Use "give," "giving," "given," and "giver" in sentences.

> Make some applesauce and share it with a friend.

> Add the suffixes "less" and "ful" to "thank." Find the meanings for these two new words in the dictionary. Print them.

> Find a recipe for turkey stuffing. Copy it. How many people will it serve?

Recipe Cards

The teacher prints simple recipes for traditional Thanksgiving dishes on file cards or colored cards.

Each card is labeled with the number of people the recipe will serve and also the number of servings the recipe is to be adapted for.

Any recipes may be altered so that the quantity of the ingredients is suitable for the children to easily multiply or divide.

The child chooses a recipe card and rewrites the recipe according to the instructions.

The child's recipes may be printed in a booklet or placed in a file box under his or her name.

Autumn Soup: 2 servings

½ lb. stewing beef, cubed   1 tsp. salt
½ c. chopped onions   ¼ tsp. pepper
2 c. water   1 bay leaf, crumbled
⅔ c. diced celery   ½ tsp. basil
⅔ c. diced potatoes   3 whole tomatoes, fresh

Write this recipe for 1 serving.

Bread Stuffing: will stuff a 4 lb. fowl

⅓ c. butter, melted   1 tsp. salt
¼ c. minced onion   ¼ tsp. pepper
4 c. bread crumbs   1 tsp. sage
½ c. chopped celery   1 tsp. thyme
½ c. chopped mushrooms   1 tsp. poultry seasoning

Write this recipe for a 12 lb. fowl.

BOOKLETS

Children like to take booklets home to show to their friends and family.

A booklet for this special day would allow the children to share their thoughts of Thanksgiving.

Topics for individual booklets could include:

Thanksgiving Long Ago

Thanksgiving Today

Things We're Thankful For

A Thanksgiving Feast

Sharing With Others

Harvest Time

Family Activities of Today and Long Ago

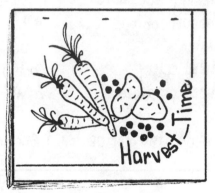

GAMES AND ACTIVITIES

Collages

Topics for the collages could include:

We're thankful for . . .

Thanks to . . .

Sharing is . . .

These collages can be made by individual children, small groups, or the whole class.

The size of the collages will depend on the number of children undertaking this activity.

Pictures for the collages can be child-drawn, cut from magazines or newspapers, photographs taken by the children, or any combination of these.

The children should also be encouraged to cut out or use words and short phrases, and to group the words and pictures in an interesting manner.

The Pilgrims Sailed

This is a circle game in which the children take turns completing the statement: "The Pilgrims sailed in their ships and when they landed, they saw ..."

The first child may choose any word to complete the statement. The next child completes the statement with a word that begins with the same letter as the first word ended with, and so on.

Turns may be taken:

> in rotation around the circle
>
> by the first child choosing the next
>
> with the teacher choosing the first child to raise his or her hand

If a child cannot respond, another child is chosen and the game proceeds.

Thoughtful Spins

Many days before Thanksgiving, the teacher and the children discuss their school and all the facilities and activities it has to offer.

Together, they compose a list of four or five thoughtful ways of showing they are thankful for having the opportunity of going to the school. The teacher prints and displays this list.

The thoughtful list could include:

> tidying the classroom and watering the plants
>
> putting books away or straightening the bookshelves in the library
>
> cleaning up the lunchroom

picking up litter on the school-grounds

making a thank you card for a staff member who has been helpful

The teacher then draws a large circle on a piece of cardboard, divides the circle into sections, and prints three or four children's names in each section.

An arrow is affixed with a paper fastener to the center of the circle.

Each day the teacher begins this activity by spinning the arrow.

When the arrow points to a group of names, these children are responsible for doing as many things on the thoughtful list as possible.

If the arrow points to a group of children who have already had a turn, the arrow is spun again.

By Thanksgiving, everyone in the class will have had a turn to show their appreciation for the school.

With older children, the teacher could print one name on each segment of the circle.

Picto-Story

Children will have fun decoding this story by drawing their own pictures in the open spaces according to the given context clues.

The teacher may want to give the children an illustrated picto-story, where they can determine the context by reading the text and the pictures.

Stories such as this can be used to stimulate interest in a topic and to encourage the creation of group or individual picto-stories.

A Pilgrim family came to America on a _____ . They lived in a _____ , in the middle of a big _____ . They had a little boy named _____ . _____ day, _____ went for a walk in the _____ to find a pumpkin. After a while, _____ wanted to go back to his _____ but he could not find his way through the _____. _____ looked in the river, but the _____ could not help him. He looked in a nest and asked the baby _____ , but they could not help him. _____ looked in a dark cave, but the sleepy _____ could not help him. Poor little _____ began to cry. Soon, _____ opened his eyes and _____ his good friend, Little _____ standing beside him. Little _____ knew how to find his way through the _____ . He could follow the sun, the stars, the _____ in the sky, or the tracks on the ground. Little _____ took _____ and led him right back to his _____ , and _____ gave Little _____ his best _____ to say ''thank you''.

Sharing

The following activities can help the children develop and spread the Thanksgiving spirit of giving, sharing, and thoughtfulness:

> gathering a class food package for a less fortunate family
>
> visiting the elderly in homes or hospitals and singing, taking paintings, or making other hand-made articles for them
>
> making milk carton, wooden, or pine cone bird feeders to provide the birds with winter food

---

Thanksgiving Luncheon

Invite parents of varying ethnic backgrounds to assist in the preparation of a Thanksgiving luncheon.

Each parent and a small group of children may work cooperatively to prepare one ethnic dish.

The preparation may be done in the homes of the assisting parents or in the school, if sufficient facilities are available.

The luncheon may then be served in the classroom with parents and children sharing and sampling the various dishes.

Recipe Books

Recipes used for the luncheon and other favorite recipes of the children are brought to school.

The children copy these recipes directly onto mimeo paper. (They may wish to add small drawings.)

The mimeos are then duplicated and the duplicated sheets are stapled together. A front and a back cover are added.

The children decorate the covers and take the recipe books home for their families.

Centers or Corners

Some suggestions are:

pioneer home

frontier general store

sand, for making a display of a pioneer village

hobbies, stressing pioneer crafts

construction, using building blocks, Popsicle sticks, logs, and bricks of various sizes

cooking, using simple ethnic recipes and parent helpers

carpentry

Centers or corners can be constructed using corrugated cardboard, boxes, rough boards, and shelving materials.

Hats and simple paper or fabric costumes can be made to enhance the work and role-playing in all centers.

Equipment and articles to stock the store, house, and other centers can be brought by the children or salvaged from store or home discards.

Centers are enhanced by the addition of curtains and roofs. Curtains can be painted on windows, made of crepe paper, or sewn from fabric. Curtains from cotton fabric are, for many reasons, more durable and can be easily made. Check bargain and remnant stores for inexpensive fabric, or your own school's supplies — large allotments are often requisitioned for crafts and stitchery. Using the selvage edges as the sides of the curtain panels, tear the fabric to the correct length. Allow for a small hem and casing which are hand or machine sewn by you or your students. (No finishing is needed, just fold over the fabric and stitch) Wire or cord is threaded through the casing for hanging.

Long, wide strips of crepe paper, rolls of colored paper, or child-made banners produce attractive roofs. They can be hung down from ceilings, arches, or hoops. Or they can be attached to a wall and slung out and down over a suspended wire.

Tail Feathers

Several turkeys may be drawn on a large sheet of paper and mounted on the bulletin board.

Each turkey has a number printed on its wing.

A box containing tail feathers is placed near the turkeys; each feather is labeled with a number.

Working on one turkey at a time, a child should choose and pin on enough tail feathers to total the number on the turkey's wing.

HANDWORK

Turkeys

PAPER PLATE TURKEY

One-half of a small, colored paper plate is scalloped around the edge. This forms the turkey's tail feathers.

A paper circle body is glued on.

A paper strip is accordion folded and glued to the middle of the paper circle to form a neck.

The turkey's head is glued to the neck.

Feet are attached to the bottom edge of the paper plate.

This turkey is effective in displays since his head wobbles.

MOSAIC TURKEY

Each child draws the outline of a turkey.

Then, after spreading glue on small areas of the turkey shape, tiny, brightly colored paper squares are applied.

Paper strips are glued on and curled to form the wing and tail feathers.

Since many, many strips and squares will be needed for an effective result, cut them on the paper cutter so that they are ready for the children's use.

Murals

Small group or class murals can be created based on the following themes:

Thanksgiving
harvesting the crops
our Thanksgiving luncheon
transportation then and now
settlements versus cities
family chores in a settlement
schools of today and long ago
Thanksgiving at my house
I could share . . .

46

Each child can be assigned a particular item or section to paint or crayon on the mural.

After the mural has been displayed, it can be cut into sections and each child can take home one section.

Wondering where to place captions or stories on completed murals or large paintings? If you fold the paper back about four inches (ten centimeters) from the bottom before the children begin their work, you will have a clean, free surface on which to record any commentary.

When large sheets are ready to go home, roll and fasten them with elastic bands, precut string, or napkin rings cut from paper rolls.

Samplers

Using burlap, tapestry needles, and scraps of different colored wool, the children may create decorative centerpiece mats to take home as a gift for the whole family.

After discussions about the Pilgrims and the lifestyles of the early settlers, the children may want to incorporate some of the following ideas into their samplers:

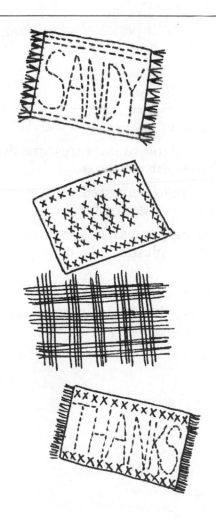

Fringe the edges.

Do simple designs using the basic cross-stitch.

Embroider or stitch their family name, or a word that signifies being thankful.

Appliqué or embroider Thanksgiving motifs.

Make a pattern by carefully pulling out threads of the burlap.

Instead of taking the samplers home, they can be sewn together or joined with fusible webbing to make a wall hanging or a special rug to sit on while reading books or listening to taped stories or music. When complete it will resemble the patchwork quilts made by the early settlers.

Trace-a-Friend

Pairs of children take turns tracing each other.

Features and pioneer dress or ethnic costumes are added, and the figure is colored or painted.

The figures are then cut out and displayed in the hallway or in class centers. (See GAMES AND ACTIVITIES, p. 44.)

A variety of poses makes for a more interesting display.

Seed Pictures

Simple designs or pictures are drawn on lightweight cardboard.

A small area is covered with glue and the seeds are attached.

This gluing process is continued until the entire picture is covered with seeds.

An assortment of seeds is used. These could include: rice, barley, popcorn kernels, split peas, and beans.

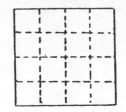

Folded-Paper Log Cabin

Fold 8″ x 8″ (20cm x 20cm) construction paper, as shown.

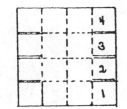

Cut on double lines, as shown.

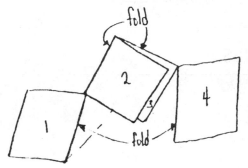

Fold flaps 2 and 3 together so they match and overlap; paste.

Fold and paste flaps 1 and 4 on top.

Paste and fold the opposite side in the same way; the side view will be as shown.

Windows and doors may be cut and folded.

A chimney, porch, fence, and other details may be added.

The finished log cabins can be a part of a pioneer village on a display table.

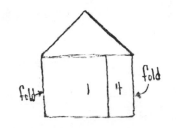

Inhabitants for the pioneer village can be made by cutting figures from catalogues and mounting them on cardboard. The figures can be dressed in clothes designed and drawn by the children. They will stand in the pioneer village when placed in a small piece of plasticene.

Evergreens

From a square of green construction paper fold and glue a paper cone. Cut away the excess paper so it will stand.

Glue on branches made from curled strips or loops of green paper.

Place the trees in the pioneer village.

Teepees, Indians, and Pilgrims can also be made from paper cones and will add interest to the pioneer village.

DRAMATICS AND PHYSICAL ACTIVITIES

You Were There

Pantomime or drama can result from the following thematic suggestions:

> a flock of turkeys
>
> planting and tending crops
>
> autumn harvest
>
> a Thanksgiving dinner
>
> constructing a log cabin
>
> an Indian scouting party
>
> an Indian celebration
>
> some pioneer chores
>
> moving over land
>
> moving along the waterways

Run, Little Turkeys

This game is played while the children sing the following verse to the tune of ''Ten Little Indians'':

> *One little, two little, three little pilgrims*
> *Looking all around just to find some turkeys.*
> *They see three and try to catch them . . .*
> *Run, little turkeys, run!*

The teacher chooses three Pilgrims who walk around the outside of a circle of children searching for some turkeys.

As the children sing "they see three," the Pilgrims each tag one child on the back.

These tagged children become the turkeys and they run clockwise around the outside of the circle.

The Pilgrims run in the opposite direction in an attempt to beat the turkeys back to their places.

Those children left without a place in the circle become the Pilgrims for the next game.

WORKSHEETS

Page 52, 53
Fill-Ins Arithmetic equations, or phonetic or language word tasks, are printed on these sheets before duplicating.

Page 54
Maze The children help the hikers through the forest to find the turkey.

Page 55
A House is a House The children compare and contrast modern homes and furnishings with those of the early settlers by drawing and/or labeling articles used in the homes.

Page 56
Symmetry The other half of the Pilgrim is drawn by the child. The figure can then be colored, cut out, and pasted onto a mural or collage.

Page 57
Turkey Tracings The child traces over the dotted lines with a pencil or crayon. The traced turkey can then be colored and, if you wish, cut out.

Page 58
A Thanksgiving Feast The child must look across and down to find and circle the hidden words.

Page 59
Things Harvested in Autumn Drawings or pictures cut from magazines are used to complete this worksheet.

Page 60
Pilgrim Pastimes The children can research and write a story of life in an early settlement; an account of the daily tasks of a Pilgrim; or a portrayal of themselves as Pilgrim children.

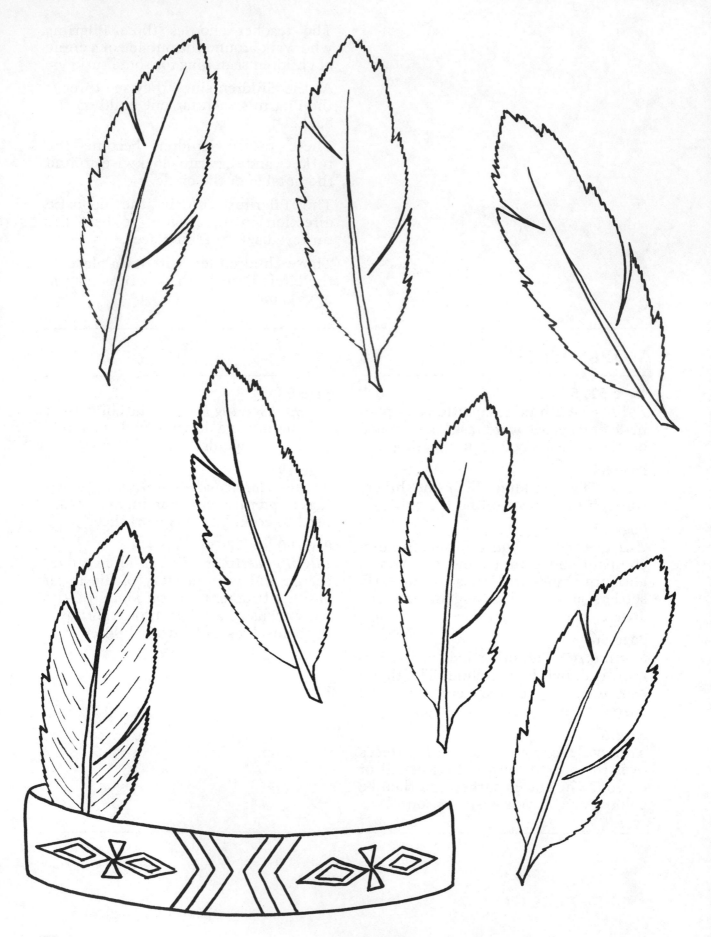

52

Will the hikers discover the turkey?

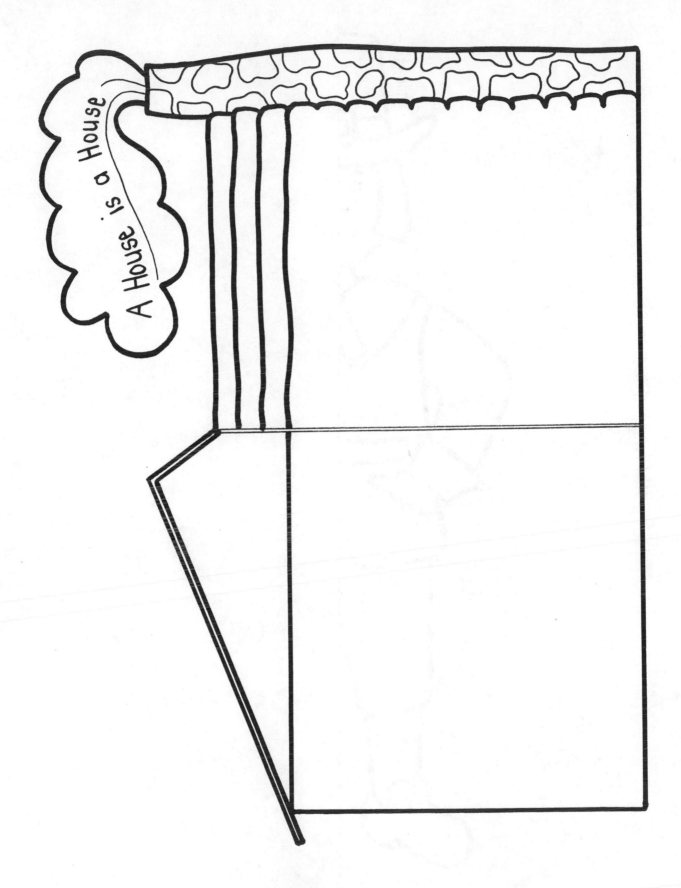

A House is a House

55

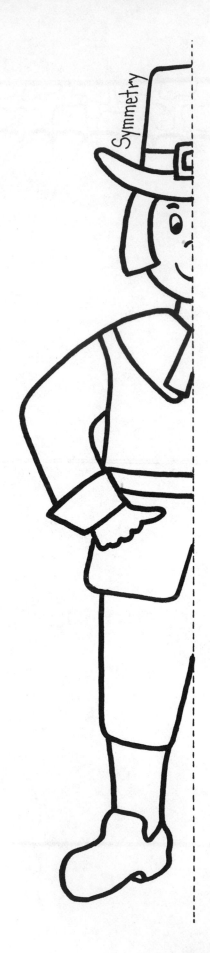

Symmetry

Turkey Tracings

Trace on the dotted lines.

Give the turkey colorful feathers.

A THANKSGIVING FEAST

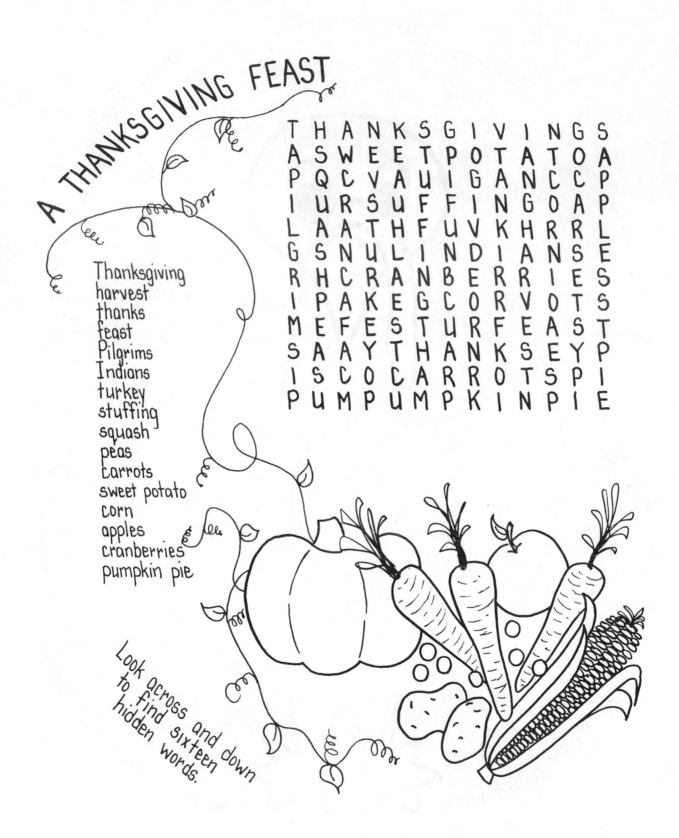

Thanksgiving
harvest
thanks
feast
Pilgrims
Indians
turkey
stuffing
squash
peas
carrots
sweet potato
corn
apples
cranberries
pumpkin pie

Look across and down to find sixteen hidden words.

```
T  H  A  N  K  S  G  I  V  I  N  G  S
A  S  W  E  E  T  P  O  T  A  T  O  A
P  Q  C  V  A  U  I  G  A  N  C  C  P
I  L  A  R  S  U  F  F  U  V  D  A  P
L  G  R  S  U  T  F  I  V  D  K  R  L
G  R  H  C  R  A  N  B  E  R  N  R  E
R  I  P  A  K  E  G  C  O  R  N  I  S
I  M  E  F  E  S  T  U  R  R  F  O  S
M  S  A  A  Y  T  H  A  N  K  S  E  T
S  I  S  C  O  C  A  R  R  O  T  S  P
P  U  M  P  U  M  P  K  I  N  P  I  E
```

58

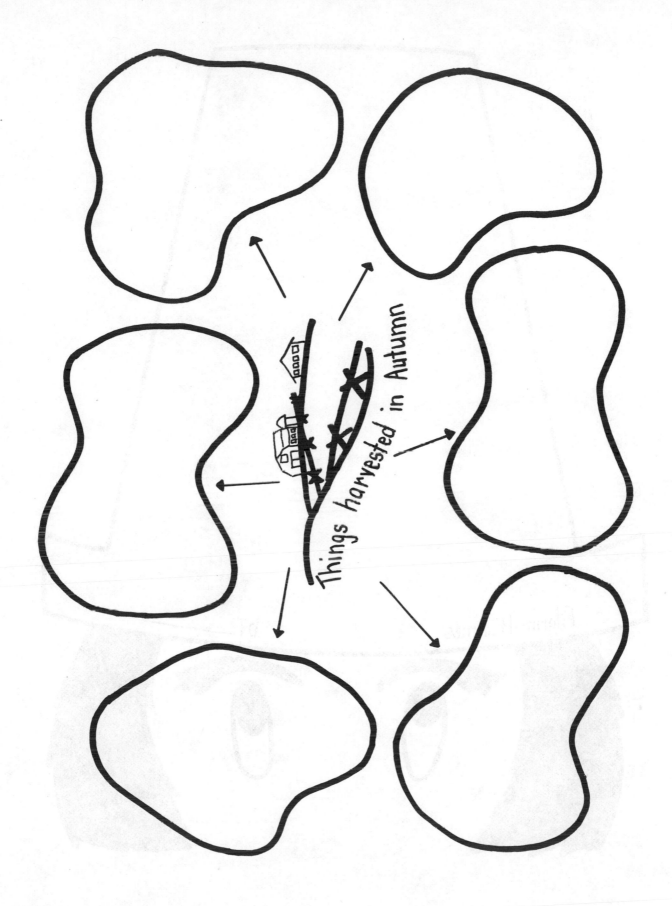

Things harvested in Autumn

Pilgrim Pastimes by _____

BOOK LIST

Alcott, Louisa May. *An Old-Fashioned Thanksgiving*. New York: J. B. Lippincott Co., 1974.

Balian, Lorna. *Sometimes It's Turkey, Sometimes It's Feathers*. New York: Abingdon Press, 1973.

Dalgliesh, Alice. *The Thanksgiving Story*. New York: Charles Scribner's Sons, 1954.

Devlin, Wende Harry. *Cranberry Thanksgiving*. New York: Parent's Magazine Press, 1971.

Glovach, Linda. *The Little Witch's Thanksgiving Book*. Englewood Cliffs, New Jersey: Prentice-Hall, 1976.

Janice. *Little Bear's Thanksgiving*. New York: Lothrop, Lee, and Shepard Co., 1967.

Ott, John. *Peter Pumpkin*. Garden City, New York: Doubleday, 1963.

Schulz, Charles M. *Charlie Brown Thanksgiving*. New York: Random House, 1974.

Tresselt, Alvin. *Autumn Harvest*. New York: Lothrop, Lee, and Shepard Co., 1966.

Weisgard, Leonard. *The Plymouth Thanksgiving*. New York: Doubleday, 1967.

Williams, Barbara. *Chester Chipmunk's Thanksgiving*. New York: E. P. Dutton, 1978.

Teacher's Resource Book:

Barth, Edna. *Turkeys, Pilgrims and Indian Corn: The Story of the Thanksgiving Symbols*. New York: Seabury Press, 1975.

CHRISTMAS

WORKCARD SETS

Graph-Pics
Trim-a-Tree
Twelve Days of Christmas

BOOKLETS

GAMES AND ACTIVITIES

Guesstimate
Watch and Do
Light Up My Tree
Sleighride
Christmas Dominoes
Stocking Fillers
On the First Day of Christmas
Countdown to Christmas
Santa's Sack
Santa Spinner
Mitten Match
Christmas Crafts

HANDWORK

Circle Bauble
Glittering Trees
Jolly Santa
Felt Christmas Stockings
Santa's Reindeer
Twinkling Christmas Trees
Marshmallow Snowman
Enchanted Elves
Christmas Wrapping Paper

DRAMATICS AND PHYSICAL ACTIVITIES

'Twas the Night Before
    Christmas
Ethnic Dances
Action Christmas

WORKSHEETS

Count and Cross
Complete, Color, Cut
Letter to Santa
Twelve Days of Christmas
Christmas Puzzle
Stocking Cap
Surprise Package
Toys!
Christmas Is . . .
Mitten Math

BOOK LIST

WORKCARD SETS

Graph-Pics

This involves a set of workcards in which each card contains a graph.

The children must accurately interpret each graph by drawing the number of each object given.

For example, the drawing for lights on the house would show eighteen yellow lights, seven green lights, and eleven blue lights.

Each card is the shape of what its graph depicts, and all types of graphs should be used.

Some Graph-Pics ideas include:

    a decorated Christmas tree

    a decorated house

    a sleigh full of toys

    a Christmas stocking

    a festive wreath

    a tree with presents underneath

    a dinner table

    a cookie plate

    a Christmas play on a stage

    a candy jar

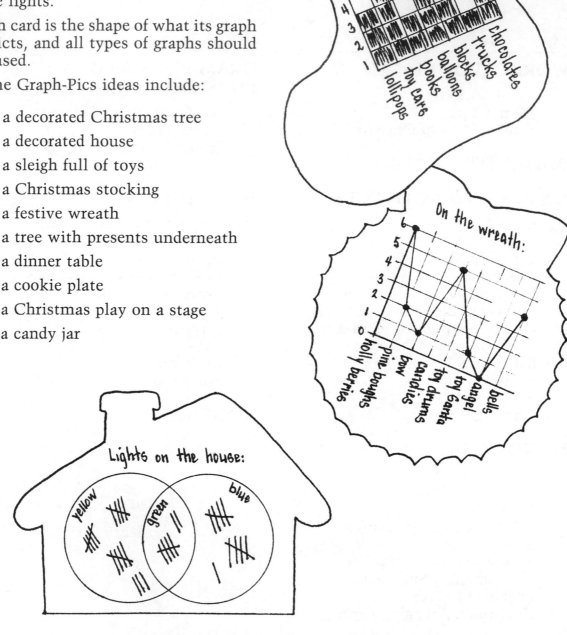

Trim-a-Tree

A set of cards, each shaped and designed as a Christmas symbol, is paper-clipped onto a large pine bough, an artificial Christmas tree, or a paper or cardboard Christmas tree.

The children choose the cards they wish to make, trace around the shape, and carefully duplicate the patterns and designs. (The amount of detail should be varied to suit a wide range of abilities.)

Examples of suitable Christmas symbols are: a stocking, a bell, a candy cane, a wreath, or a present.

Twelve Days of Christmas

A twelve-day wall calendar may be made from colorful heavy paper or cardboard.

A Christmas picture may be drawn or pasted on the top section.

A paper clip should be fastened to each of the twelve numbered squares.

The workcards are similarly numbered and clipped onto the wall calendar. (The numbers enable the teacher to easily record the work completed by each child.)

The workcards in this set include:

1. Think of one nice thing you could do at home on each of the twelve days of Christmas.

2. If you could plan the dinner for each of the twelve days of Christmas, what would you have?

3. Think of twelve people who deserve a special card or little gift for Christmas. Why is each person deserving?

4. Think of twelve ways that you could help someone in your family or neighborhood.

5. What do you think are the twelve best things about Christmas?

6. If you could choose to go somewhere on each of the twelve days of Christmas, where would you go?

7. What chores and activities might your family do on the twelve days of Christmas?

8. Think of twelve words that begin with each letter in Christmas Eve.

9. Think of twelve decorations you might find on a Christmas tree.

10. Can you think of twelve possible dangers to avoid during the Christmas season?

11. Write a Christmas poem. It should have at least twelve lines.

12. Write at least twelve equations that equal twelve. Use $+$, $-$, $\times$, $\div$, and fractions.

A matching worksheet can be made on which the child may print each of his or her twelve answers for a workcard (*see* WORKSHEETS, p. 90). Twelve of these worksheets may be stapled together with a cover forming a booklet for use with the workcard set.

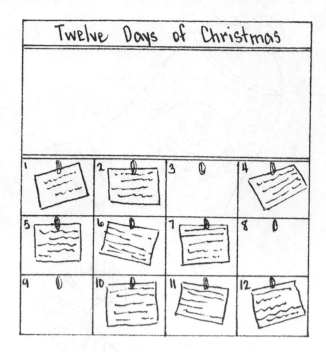

Christmas cards received in previous years can make a colorful and valuable aid to written assignments. Cut, label, and mount the pictures to produce a holiday word cache.

Used cards from other special days and occasions or inexpensive cut-outs can likewise form handy word cache charts. Or perhaps you'd prefer the children to create the chart by labelling their own drawings.

BOOKLETS

Class or individual booklets can be created using a combination of words and drawn, painted, or cut pictures.

Booklets with pages of large pieces of colored paper are especially nice at Christmas.

Some suggestions for Christmas booklets are:

Thoughts of Christmas

Christmas at Its Best

Santa's Workshop

My One Wish at Christmas Is . . .

Our Trip to See Santa Claus

Christmas in My Home

Inside Santa's Sack

Christmas Lights

Around the World at Christmas

The Night Before Christmas

Premade booklets are invaluable in the classroom. Newsprint booklets with colorful construction paper covers can be quickly cut on the paper cutter. Make your booklets in a variety of shapes and sizes, with as many or as few pages as you wish. Fasten them together with staples, string or yarn ties, rings, or accordian-fold a long strip of paper and attach the covers at each end.

Booklets can be used for projects, story writing, dictionaries, record books, diaries, drawings, practice books, and small notebooks.

GAMES AND ACTIVITIES

Guesstimate

The teacher provides two piles of cards; the item cards show a gift item and its price, and the money cards indicate a specific amount of money.

The teacher cuts out the items and their prices from Christmas catalogues or newspaper ads.

Two players alternate in drawing one card from each pile.

The player who draws the cards must quickly estimate how many of that particular item he or she can buy with the amount shown on the money card.

At the end of each turn, the item and money cards go back to the bottom of the piles.

The player awaiting a turn has a duty to correct the other player.

The players keep a tally of their correct guesstimates.

Watch and Do

The teacher cuts stars, stockings, bells, or wreaths from one, two, or three colors of construction paper.

Working with a small group, the teacher places these shapes in sequences or patterns (for example, stocking, bell, stocking, bell; star, wreath, star, bell, star, wreath, star, bell; or blue bell, red stocking, blue bell, red stocking).

Individual children then imitate what the teacher has done by choosing the correct articles and reproducing the sequences and patterns.

Light Up My Tree

Christmas trees are cut from a piece of pegboard. Then colored pegs are placed in containers next to the tree. Each color has an assigned numerical value.

The holes are labeled with arithmetic equations.

The answers to the equations are printed on the back.

The child completes the equations and lights up the tree by placing the correct pegs in the holes.

The board can be turned over and checked by the child.

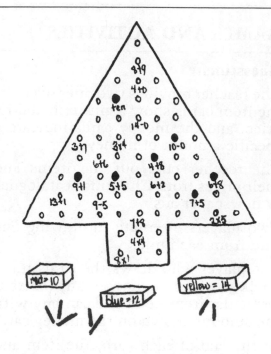

Sleighride

The children are seated on chairs that have been placed in rows as in a sleigh.

One child is the driver and has the number, equation, or phonetic sound cards.

Another child is the unseated passenger who walks around the sleigh and stops beside a seated child.

The driver holds up one card; the unseated passenger and the child he or she is standing beside race to respond.

If the unseated passenger gives the correct number, answer, or word first, he or she sits in the passenger's seat; if not, he or she goes to stand beside another child and tries again.

Christmas Dominoes

The teacher prints Christmas words on strips of cardboard.

The children try to fit all the words into a domino pattern by placing like letters beside each other.

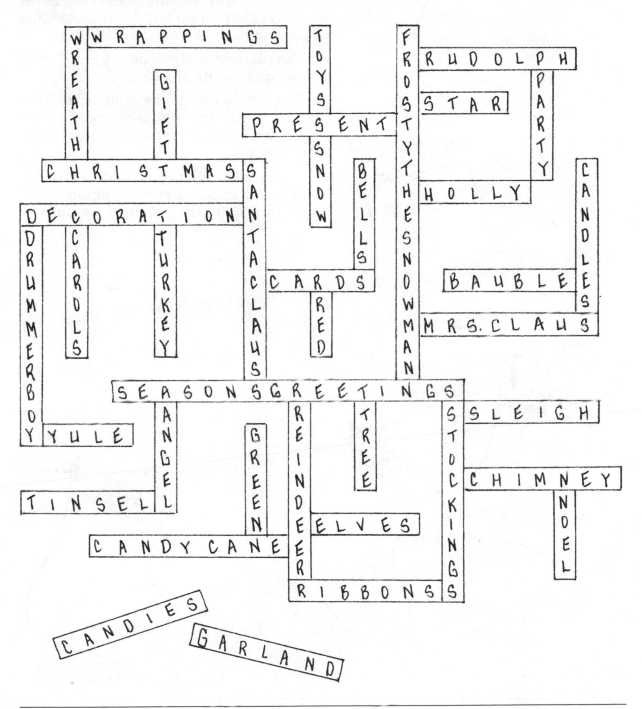

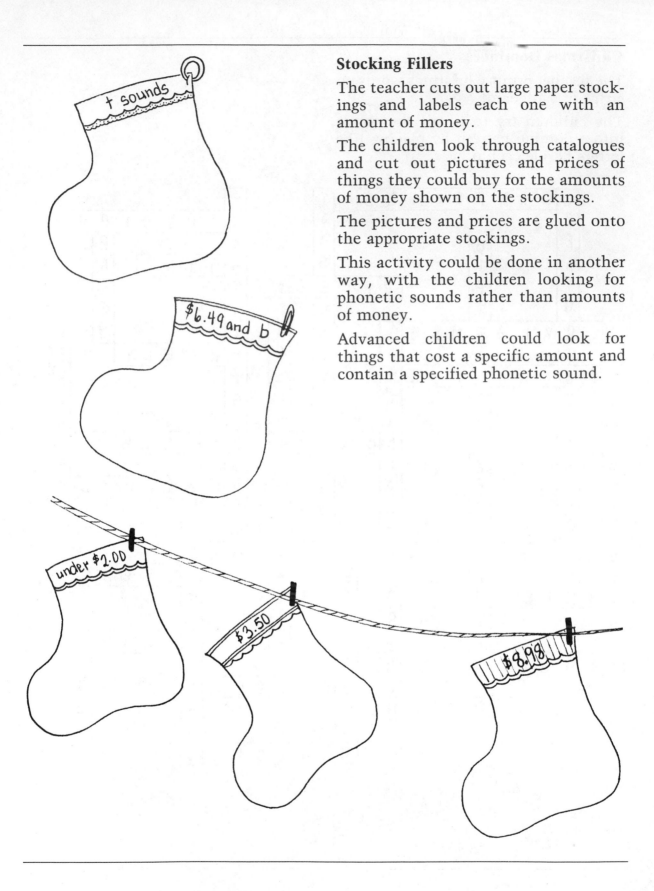

Stocking Fillers

The teacher cuts out large paper stockings and labels each one with an amount of money.

The children look through catalogues and cut out pictures and prices of things they could buy for the amounts of money shown on the stockings.

The pictures and prices are glued onto the appropriate stockings.

This activity could be done in another way, with the children looking for phonetic sounds rather than amounts of money.

Advanced children could look for things that cost a specific amount and contain a specified phonetic sound.

On the First Day of Christmas . . .

This game may be played with a small group or a whole class.

The children sit in a circle. One child begins by saying, "On the first day of Christmas, my family gave to me . . ."

The game proceeds in progression to the twelfth child, each player repeating exactly what has been said and adding his or her own thought. However, if a mistake or omission is made, the first child to raise his or her hand is allowed to begin the game again with , "On the first day of Christmas, my family gave to me . . ."

Countdown to Christmas

The children each cut out twenty-five small Christmas shapes, punch two holes in each shape, and tie the shapes together with wool.

Beginning on December 1st, each day one shape is untied and is taken home where the chain may be reassembled in the reverse way.

Each shape may have the date printed on it.

Santa's Sack

The teacher makes a Santa's Sack which holds one of the following activities.

The teacher may wish to use only one of these activities or may wish to prepare many of them and surprise the children with the contents of Santa's Sack.

CHRISTMAS WORDS

The whole class works together to compile a list of Christmas words.

The children choose two or three of the words and use them in a sentence, or choose ten words and list them in alphabetical order.

The word list could include: Christmas, Santa Claus, tree, angel, beautiful, decorations, ribbons, colorful, baubles, lights, sparkling, delicious, elves, peaceful, stockings, Rudolph, angelic, cards, tinsel, twinkling, candies, reindeer, red, turkey, yuletide, green, drummerboy, toys, snowy, star, joy, Frosty the Snowman, candy cane, wreath, sleigh, bells, gifts, chimney, wrappings, Mrs. Claus, presents, carols, holly, shiny, season's greetings, and friends.

CHARACTER PUPPETS

An assortment of hand puppets or child-made stick, or paperbag puppets may be used for this activity.

The children could use the puppets:

> for impromptu dramatics or a planned and rehearsed Christmas play

> as the basic characters for written stories

Children greatly enjoy reading to puppets. Place the puppets in a reading corner or library center to encourage oral or silent reading. Having worked with the puppets in other activities, children will be quick to adopt these new friends. Stuffed animals, dolls, or live pets also make fine reading partners, especially when given distinctive names or characteristics.

CHARACTER CARDS

The teacher prints the names of the following fictional characters on cards: Santa, Mrs. Claus, enchanted elf, Rudolph, ice monster, Frosty the Snowman, sleigh stealer, Willy Walrus, child-napper, Santa's lazy helper, little boy, splendiferous sleigh, daredevil dog, Santa's pet seal, little girl, and master toymaker.

Three or more cards are chosen and a story is written involving these characters.

These may be in the form of:

> individual stories
>
> chart stories written by a group
>
> continuing stories where each child adds a sentence
>
> picture stories or cartoons

To add variety, the children could record any of the above stories on tape, perhaps adding their own dialogue and music.

ALPHABET CARDS

The children may pull out a handful of letters and use them to make as many Christmas words as possible.

MONEY CARDS

The children pull out money cards and determine how much money they will have after they buy the item mentioned on the card.

The amounts of money and the number of purchases on any one card may be increased to make this activity more difficult.

Money cards may be used for practicing mental addition. The children add up the cost of each item and tell how much money they have spent.

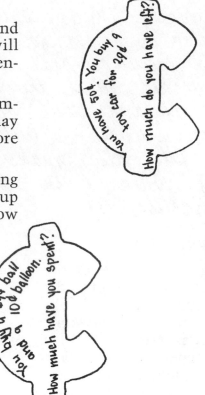

Santa Spinner

Two to four players participate.

The arrow points to places on the gameboard indicating people receiving a Christmas gift.

Players take turns spinning Santa's arm and quickly naming an appropriate gift for the person the arrow points to.

Players awaiting their turns judge the appropriateness of the gift named.

If a player mentions an inappropriate gift, he or she must spin again.

Mitten Match

Many pairs of decorated paper mittens provide fun and a good opportunity for visual discrimination when they are scattered and waiting to be matched.

The designs on the mittens can be very simple or intricately detailed.

Older children can use the mitten pairs to play the game Concentration. In this game, the mittens are scattered face down and two players take turns trying to find the matching pairs.

This activity could be carried out using pairs of stockings, ornaments, presents, bells, or angels.

Christmas Crafts

Parents are invited to demonstrate traditional or cultural Christmas crafts.

The crafts might include the baking of Christmas treats, the creating of home or tree decorations, the wrapping of parcels, or the making of gifts.

After demonstrations by parents, the children should be encouraged to attempt the crafts.

Have the parents and children arrange displays of the crafts.

Ask other classes in the school to visit your displays.

Have a guest book for parents or other visitors to sign. It is a handy record of events, visitations, or conferences.

HANDWORK

Circle Bauble

Each child cuts nine circles out of used Christmas cards, brightly colored wallpaper, or colored construction paper.

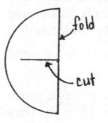

One circle is left as is; the other eight are folded in half and cut as shown.

The eight folded and cut circles are placed around the circumference of the one unfolded circle to form a bauble.

A hole is punched in the flat circle so the bauble may be hung on a tree with wool or ribbon.

Have many large needles pre-strung with yarn, string, or heavy thread and placed for easy access.

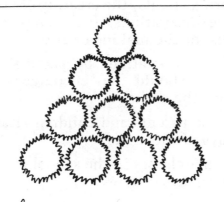

Glittering Trees

White or colored baking cups (muffin- or candy-sized) are glued to a piece of heavy paper to form a tree shape.

The frilly edges of the trees can be decorated by gluing on gold or silver glitter, tiny beads, sequins, confetti punched from foil or scraps of shiny paper, or coarse salt.

Corrugated paper makes an attractive display surface. It can be purchased in large rolls in a variety of bright colors. Your initial expenditure will be rewarded by a colorful multipurpose product which will last for several years. Corrugated paper can be stapled directly onto tackboard or walls. Cylinders of this paper can stand freely about your classroom. (Use straight pins to attach displays and preserve the corrugated surface.)

Wallpaper is another attractive, durable display material. Salvage roll ends or wallpaper books. When stapled to tackboard, the book pages provide an interesting collage effect for a display background.

Jolly Santa

Cover a toilet tissue roll with a piece of pink or white paper.

Draw or glue on jolly eyes, rosy cheeks, and a red nose in the center section of the roll.

White paper strips are curled and glued on to form the beard.

A piece of red crepe paper is rolled and tied at the top with a long piece of thread, forming Santa's stocking cap. Smaller white paper curls are glued on as the headband.

The long ends of thread at the top of Santa's hat enable you to hang your jolly Santas around the classroom, from paper chains, or on the Christmas tree.

Felt Christmas Stockings

Felt is a sturdy fabric for children to handle; the self-finishing edges eliminate the need for a sewing machine or for difficult hand stitches.

Using blunt needles threaded with wool, the children sew two stocking pieces together.

Depending on individual dexterity, children can stitch their names, embroider simple designs, attach lace or ribbons, and appliqué Christmas motifs.

Santa's Reindeer

One-and-a-half toilet tissue rolls are painted brown and fastened together to form the head and body.

Legs can be made from corks that have been split lengthwise, pipe cleaners, heavy wire, strips of paper tightly rolled, or empty thread spools.

Antlers are made by bending and attaching pipe cleaners.

Small beads or tiny lumps of plasticene form interesting facial features.

Reindeer can be displayed individually on shelves or countertops or they can be grouped together in a Christmas scene.

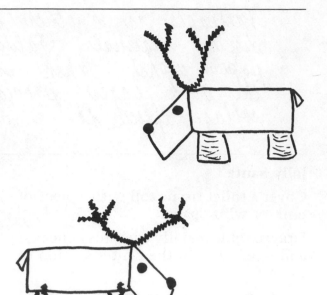

Twinkling Christmas Trees

Each child cuts two identical trees from green construction paper, holds the two trees together, and punches holes in them at random.

When enough holes have been punched, the children glue tiny pieces of different colored cellophane paper over the holes on one of their trees.

The two trees are glued together so the cellophane pieces are on the inside.

When the trees are hung near a window or around a light fixture, the cellophane lights will twinkle.

Marshmallow Snowman

Each child will need three regular-sized marshmallows, some small pieces of crepe paper, small pieces of black and brown paper, a pipe cleaner, sequins, toothpicks, and straight pins.

Two of the marshmallows should be joined using a toothpick.

The third marshmallow should be cut in half, forming two arms.

Each half should be attached to the lower body section by inserting a toothpick horizontally through the arms and body.

Sequins are then pinned to the marshmallows to make the eyes, mouth, and buttons.

A colorful scarf of crepe paper is tied on.

A pipe cleaner broom handle is wrapped tightly around a fringed and rolled piece of brown paper. The bristles are then fanned out and the broom is held by the snowman.

A circular paper brim and rolled paper crown are glued together and pinned on as a top hat.

Enchanted Elves

Felt hands, feet, eyes, nose, and vest are glued on to a large pine cone.

A fabric tassel cap and cotton batting whiskers complete the elf.

Christmas Wrapping Paper

Wrapping paper can easily be made out of tissue paper or newsprint by using the following techniques.

PRINTING

Designs and patterns are printed by dipping a variety of articles into thick paint and then pressing them down on the paper.

The amount of pressure exerted alters the impression that is made.

Children must be shown that if any sideways movement is made, the design will be blurred.

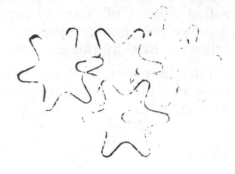

Appropriate articles to use for printing include an empty spool, a ball of twine, a piece of rope, a cork, a bottle cap, sandpaper, a tiny piece of carpet, erasers, halved cooking onions, carrots, potatoes, burlap, bamboo, a straw place-mat, a sponge, a steel wool pad, leaves, a pinecone, a piece of bark, a twig, toilet paper rolls, scraps of wool, corrugated cardboard, individual or multiple drinking straws, a child's wooden block, or Christmas shapes that have been cut from thick cardboard.

SPATTERING

Colorful paint can be spattered over an entire piece of paper or Christmas shapes can be blocked out by spattering over stencils.

Small rocks are very handy for holding the stencils in place.

Rubbing a toothbrush that has been dipped in paint over a fine screen produces an even spray of color.

BLEACHING

Cookie cutters dipped in bleach and stamped on colored tissue or newsprint create interesting effects.

DIPPING AND DYEING

Tissue paper or newsprint is folded in various ways and the corners are dipped into fairly strong solutions of food coloring or household dyes.

After the first dipping, the paper must be allowed to dry. Then, it may be refolded and dipped into another color.

This dipping and dyeing procedure is continued until a pleasing effect is achieved.

RUBBING

Designs and patterns are produced when crayons are rubbed over paper that has been placed on top of a textured surface.

BLOTTING

The children fingerpaint directly on a table top or vinyl surface using thick paint.

Newsprint is then placed on top and the paint is blotted onto the paper.

Two or three blottings can be made from each application of paint.

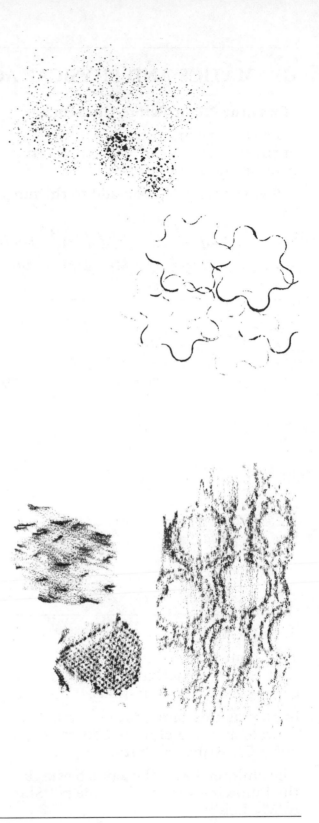

DRAMATICS AND PHYSICAL ACTIVITIES

'Twas the Night Before Christmas

This story poem, used in part or in its entirety, can lead to some fine pantomime and drama.

A few simple props can add to the fun.

Many of the traditional songs for the various holidays are also excellent for promoting improvisational dramatics.

Ethnic Dances

Dancing is an enjoyable art form in many different cultures.

The teacher and the children may learn various dances through:

> library research
>
> participation by parents or friends of differing cultural backgrounds
>
> demonstrations by local ethnic groups

The class might enjoy sharing what they have learned in a performance for other classes or for parents and friends.

Action Christmas

This game is preceded by a class discussion on the activities involved in getting ready for Christmas.

In playing this game, the children sit in a circle and one child is chosen to act out a Christmas activity.

The children begin the game by singing the following song to the tune of "Skip to My Lou":

Christmas is coming, what will we do?
Christmas is coming, what will we do?
Look at (child's name) and see what he can do
Now guess what he is doing.

The child who has been chosen then does his pantomime and the other children try to guess what he or she has done.

After three guesses the pantomime should be repeated.

When a correct guess has been made the game continues with the children singing and the child who has guessed correctly being the next actor.

WORKSHEETS

Page 87

Count and Cross The children cross out the unwanted letters by counting across and down. The remaining letters spell the Christmas message, "Santa Claus is coming to town."

Page 88

Complete, Color, Cut Arithmetic questions are printed on these seasonal shapes. The entire worksheet or individual shapes may be given to the children for completion, coloring, and cutting. They can then be displayed on a real or paper Christmas tree.

Page 89

Letter to Santa This is to be duplicated on plain, lined, or colored paper and used for writing letters or stories to Santa Claus.

Page 90

Twelve Days of Christmas See WORKCARD SETS, page 000.

Page 91

Christmas Puzzle The children cut out the pieces and fit them together. When the puzzle is solved, the Christmas tree is glued to another sheet of paper and outlined or colored. For durability, duplicate this worksheet onto construction paper or lightweight cardboard.

Similar puzzles can easily be made for other special days by cutting simple outlined figures or shapes into puzzle pieces. The difficulty of the puzzle could be determined by the size and shape of the pieces. For safekeeping, place each puzzle in its own envelope.

Page 92

Stocking Cap The picture is completed, colored, and a story is told or written.

Page 93

Surprise Package The children color the package they would choose and describe the contents in words and/or pictures.

Page 94

Toys! The children may draw the toys or cut pictures from magazines and catalogues.

Page 95

Christmas Is . . . The children show what Christmas means to them by pasting cut pictures and phrases from magazines or used Christmas cards; by drawing their own pictures and adding captions; or by writing a descriptive paragraph or poem.

Page 96

Mitten Math Duplicate this sheet onto construction paper or lightweight cardboard for greater durability. The number requiring practice is printed on the mitten. The duplicated sheet is then given to a child and he or she follows the directions on the sheet. The child can print additional facts on the blank math strip. The answers may be given orally, or they may be recorded on a chalkboard or in a notebook. Two children may use their mittens and math strips to play a game of math recall.

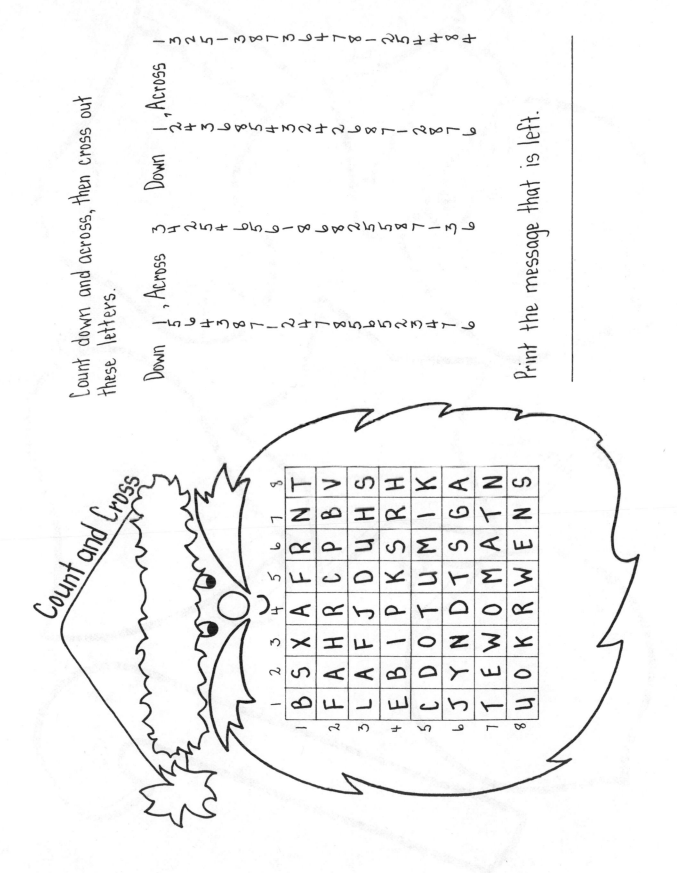

Count and Cross

Count down and across, then cross out these letters.

Down 1, Across

Down 3

Down 5, Across

Print the message that is left.

87

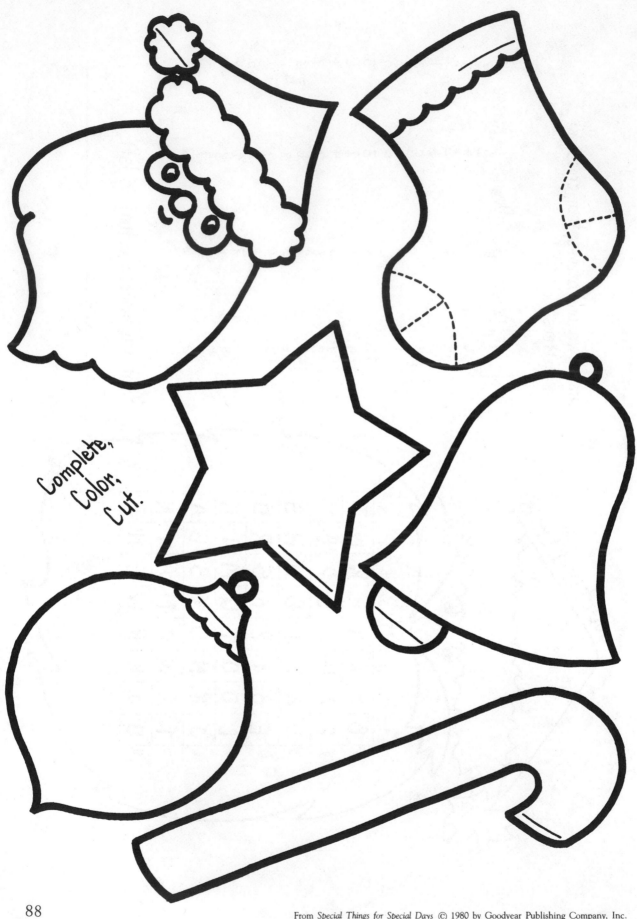

Complete, Color, Cut.

Twelve Days of Christmas

Workcard _____

1	2	3	4
5	6	7	8
9	10	11	12

Who is wearing this Stocking?

SURPRISE PACKAGE

Which package would you choose?

Describe what is inside.

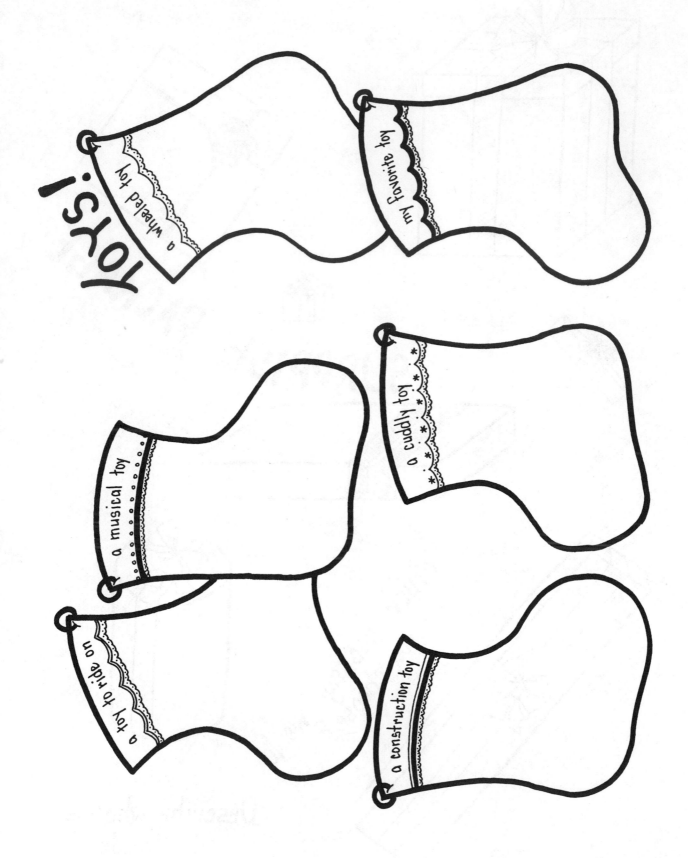

Toys!

a wheeled toy

my favorite toy

a musical toy

a cuddly toy

a toy to ride on

a construction toy

Christmas Is . . .

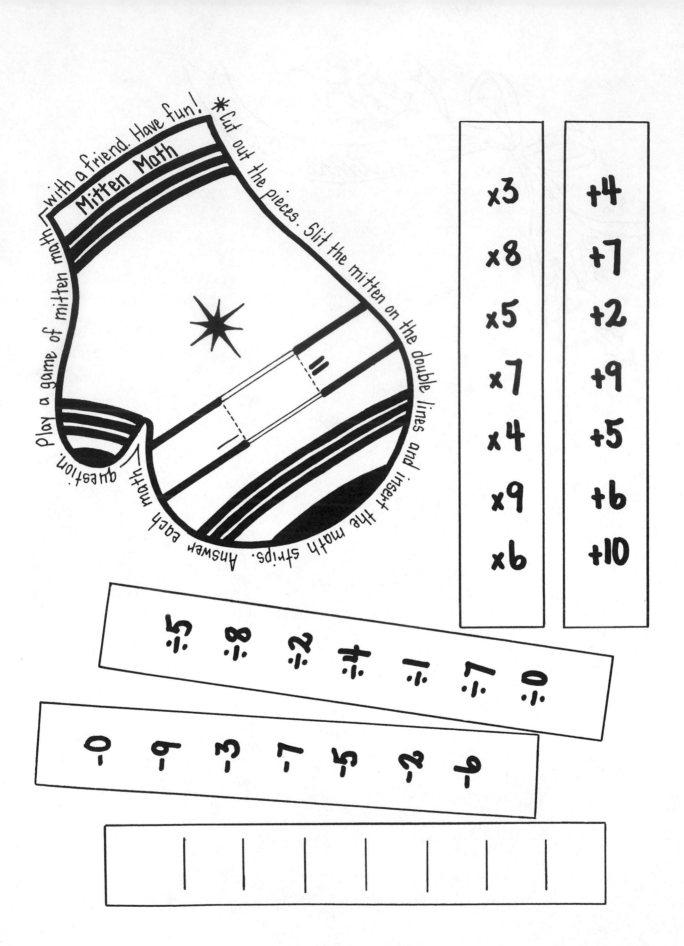

Mitten Math

Play a game of mitten math with a friend. Have fun!

* Cut out the pieces. Slit the mitten on the double lines and insert the math strips. Answer each math question.

×3 +4
×8 +7
×5 +2
×7 +9
×4 +5
×9 +6
×6 +10

÷5 ÷8 ÷2 ÷4 ÷1 ÷7 ÷0

−0 −9 −3 −1 −5 −2 −6

BOOK LIST

Adams, Adrienne. *The Christmas Party*. New York: Charles Scribner's Sons, 1978.

Andersen, Hans Christian. *The Fir Tree*. New York: Harper and Row, 1970.

Balian, Lorna. *Bah! Humbug?* Nashville: Abingdon Press, 1977.

Barry, Robert. *Mr. Willowby's Christmas Tree*. New York: McGraw-Hill, 1963.

Baum, L. Frank. *A Kidnapped Santa Claus*. New York: Bobbs-Merrill, 1969.

Bonsall, Crosby. *Twelve Bells for Santa*. New York: Harper and Row, 1977.

Briggs, Raymond. *Father Christmas*. New York: Penguin, 1973.

Briggs, Raymond. *Father Christmas Goes on Holiday*. New York: Penguin, 1975.

Bright, Robert. *Georgie's Christmas Carol*. Garden City: New York, 1975.

Carley, Wayne. *Charley the Mouse Finds Christmas*. Toronto, Ontario: Thomas Nelson and Sons, 1972.

Carrick, Carol. *Paul's Christmas Birthday*. New York: Greenwillow Books, 1978.

Darling, Kathy. *The Mystery in Santa's Toyshop*. New Canaan, Connecticut: Garrard, 1978.

de Brunhoff, Laurent. *Babar's Christmas Tree*. New York: Random House, 1974

De Lage, Ida. *ABC Christmas*. New Canaan, Connecticut: Garrard, 1978.

De Lage, Ida. *ABC Santa Claus*. New Canaan, Connecticut: Garrard, 1978.

Devlin, Wende and Harry. *Cranberry Christmas*. New York: Parents' Magazine Press, 1976.

Estes, Eleanor. *The Coat-Hanger Christmas Tree*. New York: Atheneum, 1973.

Ets, Maria Hall, and Labastida, Aurora. *Nine Days to Christmas*. New York: Viking Press, 1959.

Fenner, Carol. *Christmas Tree on the Mountain*. New York: Harcourt, Brace and World, 1966.

Foreman, Michael. *The Great Sleigh Robbery*. London: Hamish Hamilton, 1968.

Hoban, Russell. *Emmett Otter's Jug-Band Christmas*. New York: Parent's Magazine Press, 1971.

Hoff, Syd. *Where's Prancer?* New York: Harper and Row, 1965.

Hoover, Helen. *Great Wolf and the Good Woodsman*. New York: Parents' Press Magazine, 1967.

Hutchins, Pat. *The Silver Christmas Tree*. New York: Macmillan, 1974.

Hyman, Trina Schart. *How Six Found Christmas*. Boston: Little, Brown and Co., 1969.

Irion, Ruth Hershey. *The Christmas Tree Cookie*. Philadelphia: Westminster Press, 1976.

Kay, Helen. *A Stocking for a Kitten*. New York: Abeland-Schuman, 1965.

Kelley, True, and Lindblom, Steven. *The Mouses' Terrible Christmas*. New York: Lothrop, Lee, and Shepard, 1978.

Kent, Jack. *The Christmas Piñata*. New York: Parents' Magazine Press, 1975.

Kent, Jack. *Twelve Days of Christmas*. New York: Parents' Magazine Press, 1973.

Kerr, Judith, *Mog's Christmas*. London: Collins, 1976.

Knotts, Howard. *The Lost Christmas*. New York: Harcourt, Brace, Jovanovich, 1978.

Krahn, Fernando. *How Santa Claus Had a Long and Difficult Journey Delivering His Presents*. New York: Delacorte Press, 1970.

Krahn, Fernando. *The Biggest Christmas Tree on Earth*. Boston: Little Brown and Co., 1978.

Kroeber, Theodora. *A Green Christmas*. Berkeley: Parnassus Press, 1967.

Krol, Steven. *Santa's Crash-Bang Christmas*. New York: Holiday House, 1977.

Lindgren, Astrid. *Christmas In Noisy Village*. New York: Viking Press, 1963.

Low, Joseph. *The Christmas Grump*. New York: Atheneum, 1977.

Polkosnik, George. *Bluetoes: Santa's Special Helper*. Buffalo: Books Canada, 1975.

Proysen Alf. *Mrs. Pepperpot's Christmas*. London: Hutchinson Junior Books, 1970.

Richards, Jack. *Johann's Gift to Christmas*. Vancouver, Canada: J. J. Douglas Ltd., 1972.

Seuss, Dr. *How The Grinch Stole Christmas!* New York: Random House, 1957.

Wells, Rosemary. *Morris's Disappearing Bag*. New York: Dial Press, 1975.

Wildsmith, Brian. *The Twelve Days of Christmas*. New York: Franklin Watts, 1972.

Young, Chip. *Honky the Christmas Goose*. Toronto, Canada: Clarke, Irwin, and Co., 1972.

Zakhoder, Boris. *How a Piglet Crashed the Christmas Party*. New York: Lothrop, Lee, and Shepard, 1971.

Zolotow, Charlotte. *The Beautiful Christmas Tree*. Berkeley: Parnassus Press, 1972.

Valentine's Day

WORKCARD SETS

    Poem Starters
    Friendship
    Arrow Aim
    Triplets

BOOKLETS

GAMES AND ACTIVITIES

    Friendship Trail
    A Matter of Size
    Tossword
    Valentine Cookies
    Heart-Strings

HANDWORK

    Opaque Hearts
    Valentine Envelopes
    Heartlings
    Add-a-Heart
    Shiny Hearts
    Lacy Hearts
    Crowns

DRAMATICS AND PHYSICAL ACTIVITIES

    Friendship Chain
    Funny Valentines

WORKSHEETS

    Mend the Broken Hearts
    Valen-twins
    A Valentine
    My Favorites
    Heart Words
    Numbers are friends, too!
    From My Heart
    Valentines
    Jack of Hearts

BOOK LIST

Poem Starters

Children enjoy poetry and they usually find that writing their own poems is easier when they are provided with an idea to develop.

> A pretty little heart
> Colored pink and blue . . .

> I'm making a card
> And inside it will say . . .

> You are sweet and thoughtful
> You are always kind . . .

> A heart trimmed with ribbons
> Flowers and lace . . .

> When I saw you
> I knew it would be fun . . .

> A red and white heart
> Is waiting here to say . . .

> Cupid is sending
> An arrow right your way . . .

> You are my best friend
> So I will always be . . .

> I hope your day is happy
> I hope your day is fine . . .

> I'm making this card, just for you
> I'm using ribbons and pretty lace,
> too . . .

> Cupid has friendly arrows
> He shoots them from a bow . . .

> Family and friends
> And playmates, too . . .

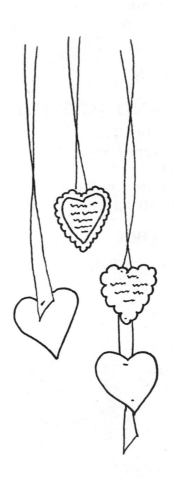

These Poem Starters are designed to stimulate creativity. For this reason, they should be presented to the children in attractive and interesting ways.

> They may be printed on hearts that are glued to paper doilies and suspended from hoops or coat hangers. The children's poems can be hung along with the Poem Starters.

They may be printed in the center of large hearts in a tackboard display. The children's poems can be added to the display.

The Poem Starters can also be attached to pink and red crepe paper streamers that are hung from the ceiling. Completed poems can also be attached to the streamers.

Trees are another excellent way of displaying hearts or any other special work. You can use a potted shrub or bare branches which have been secured in a pot containing rocks or plasticene. Workcards or completed assignments can be hung from the tree along with seasonal art work. The children have fun watching their tree change throughout the year.

Friendship

This set of workcards encourages the children to think about their friends and what friendship means.

The children could record their thoughts in writing, on a tape recorder, or through drawings, paintings or photographs.

These are some friendship topics the children may want to tell about:

one of your friends—how you met and became friends

a time you were proud of something a friend did

a time you were sad—what a friend did to help you feel happy again

a time when someone teased you—how did you feel and what did you do about it?

a time when you were afraid to do something—how did a friend help to make you feel more confident?

some happy feelings you can share with friends

some things you like to do with your best friends

how you could show your appreciation to a friend

why people need friends

When you are making workcards with a traced motif, place the work against a window. Or, scrounge a piece of plexiglass or framed glass and place this across your knees with a light shining from underneath. This method is much easier on your arms and your pens won't dry out.

Your own gummed seals can be made by tracing cartoon or coloring book characters onto gummed paper. These can be used on workcards or on special projects completed by students.

Arrow Aim

The teacher makes several heart-shaped workcards, each having a different number to aim for.

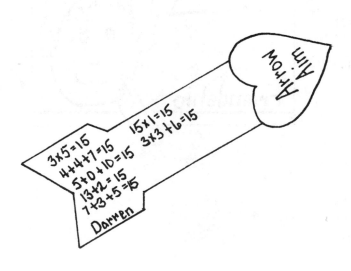

The workcards may be used individually by the children or one workcard can be displayed and assigned to a group.

The children make as many equations as they can using "+" or "×" and they print these on paper arrows.

For example, in aiming for 20 a child could print:

$10 + 10 = 20$	$4 \times 5 = 20$	$4 + 6 + 8 + 2 = 20$
$5 + 5 + 10 = 20$	$2 \times 10 = 20$	$(2+2) \times 5 = 20$
$12 + 8 = 20$	$(2 \times 5) + 10 = 20$	$4 + (4 \times 4) = 20$

A paper cutter is terrific for cutting many simple paper arrows at one time. In fact many monotonous tasks are easily and quickly accomplished on the paper cutter — trimming laminated workcards; making paper frames and labels; cutting construction paper, newsprint, egg cartons, straws, wool, paper rolls, and other materials for art work and classroom projects; making crepe paper grass and heavy paper fences for displays; cutting notebooks to half-size for pupil dictionaries, record books, or project books.

Triplets

This is a set of arithmetic workcards on which children form as many equations as they can using the three numbers on each card.

They can use "+", "−", "×", and "÷"

For example, using 3, 6, 9, a child might print:

$3 + 6 = 9$	$9 - 3 - 3 = 3$	$9 - 3 = 3 + 3$
$6 + 3 = 9$	$3 \times 3 = 9$	$3 \times 3 = 6 + 3$
$9 = 3 + 6$	$9 - 3 = 6$	$9 \div 3 = 3$
$9 = 6 + 3$	$9 - 6 = 3$	

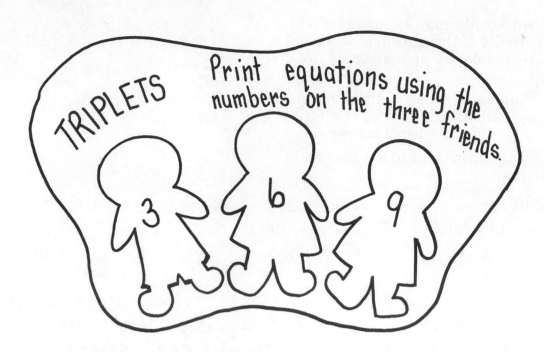

Some number combinations that could be put on workcards are: 2,5,10; 3,6,18; 3,4,12; 2,25,50; 2,4,16; 3,8,24; 2,5,20

Workcards, such as Triplets, are much more appealing when they have a design or motif on them. Instead of spending your time drawing the same motif on each workcard ～ draw the motif on a stencil and run the workcards through the duplicating machine.

BOOKLETS

These individual, child-made booklets are more fun when made from pink paper, cut in heart shapes, or cut as paper dolls:

I Love . . .

My Favorite Things . . .

My Friends . . .

A Friend is for . . .

Ways of Making Friends . . .

Showing You Care . . .

Welcoming a New Classmate . . .

You may let the children choose which topic they wish to explore, or you may give them booklets with several different pages. (See WORKSHEETS, pages 119 to 121.)

Small sanded wooden boards — either specially cut or salvaged from home building projects — make fine drawing boards or clipboards. When supplied with metal clips or clothespins these boards are excellent surfaces when working out-of-doors, on the floor, or on fact-finding visits to the library or resource center.

GAMES AND ACTIVITIES

Friendship Trail

Two to four players participate.

Each takes a turn moving one heart, rolling the two dice, and giving an equation with the numbers on the dice and the ''sign'' printed on the heart.

If a correct response is given, the player stays on the ''sign''; if not, he or she returns to the starting line.

The winner is the first to reach the two friends.

Using paper figures or toy people as markers can add to the fun.

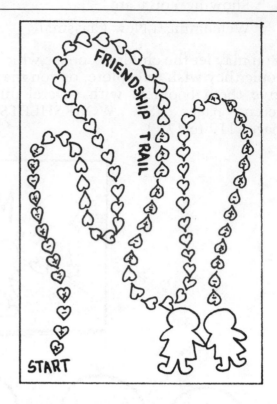

A Matter of Size

The teacher cuts paper hearts in a progression of sizes.

The children are asked to place the hearts in order, according to their size, from smallest to largest, and largest to smallest.

The children are also asked to stack the hearts in order, with the largest on the bottom.

If the teacher cuts two hearts of each size, the children can match the pairs and place each pair in order.

For a variation, this activity can be carried out with cardboard boxes that are in a progression of sizes—perhaps an object that would fit exactly inside each box could be found, giving the children the chance to order the objects and place objects in the correct boxes.

Tossword

Many adjoining hearts are drawn on a large piece of lightweight cardboard.

Each heart is labeled with a phonetic sound and the cardboard is placed on the floor.

Three bean bags are used in this tossing game.

Two to four children may play. One child tosses a bean bag and the others race to respond with a word containing the correct phonetic sound.

The child tossing has three turns before passing the bean bags to the next player.

The time limit for this game should be set before the children begin to play.

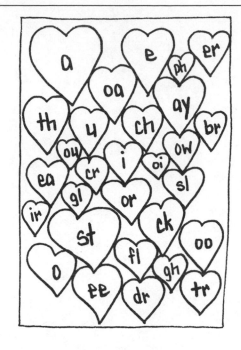

Making games takes time so durability is important. All paper or cardboard games should be laminated or covered with clear, adhesive vinyl. For variation and ease of storage, games can be drawn onto oilcloth, vinyl, felt, or canvas using indelible ink markers. These will withstand constant use and they can be rolled or folded when you are finished with them.

Valentine Cookies

These sugar cookies are easy to make and the children will have fun decorating their edible Valentines.

    1½ cups (340 ml) icing sugar
    1 cup (227 ml) margarine
    1 egg
    1 tsp. (5 ml) vanilla
    2½ cups (567 ml) sifted flour
    1 tsp. (5 ml) baking soda

Blend sugar and butter. Then, mix in egg and flavoring.

Stir in dry ingredients.

Refrigerate for at least 2 hours.

Divide cookie dough into small portions and allow children to roll out dough on a floured surface.

Heart shapes are cut from dough using cookie cutters that have been dipped in flour.

Place on lightly greased baking sheets and bake for approximately 8 minutes at 375° F. (190° C).

This recipe makes 4 to 5 dozen heart-shaped cookies.

To decorate their cookies, the children may:

sprinkle on colored sugar decorations before baking

squeeze tinted butter icing from paper tubes onto the baked and cooled cookies

spread with a tinted icing sugar glaze

When having a snack or a party on these special days, it would be fun for the children to select foods of a particular color. For example, on Valentines Day some of the choices could include red foods such as tomatoes, sweet red peppers, pomegranates, cherries, strawberries, raspberry jello, and cinnamon candy hearts.

Heart-Strings

The teacher cuts many pieces of brightly colored wool and attaches a numbered paper heart to one end.

The children are instructed to look at the heart and string the correct number of objects onto the wool.

For stringing, the children may use paper hearts, wooden or plastic beads, drinking straws that have been cut into short sections, empty thread spools, or macaroni.

Completed Heart-Strings could be:

> worn by the children
>
> displayed on a tackboard
>
> suspended from hoops or doorways

HANDWORK

Opaque Hearts

On a piece of white bond paper, draw a design using vivid colored crayons and pressing heavily.

When the paper is completely colored, lay the crayon side down on newspaper and iron with a hot iron.

Using a piece of red, pink, purple, or blue construction paper, cut a large heart shape from the middle.

Glue or staple the construction paper frame to the uncrayoned side of the heart.

To mount on a window, place pieces of rolled masking tape on the frame so that the crayoned side will be against the window.

Opaque hearts make an effective display, as the light from the window will shine through.

Rectangular or square frames can easily be made on the paper cutter by folding colored construction paper in half and cutting out the mid-section as shown:

fold

cutting lines

Frame widths of approximately 1½ inches (3 cm) are the most usable. And don't forget to save the center sections. They can be used to make additional frames or in art work assignments. Cut a number of frames of various colors and sizes so they are ready when the need arises.

Valentine Envelopes

Each child cuts two identical hearts from construction paper and, holding the two hearts together, punches holes around the edge as shown.

The child sews in and out of each hole using a tapestry needle and brightly colored wool.

The heart envelopes may be decorated by gluing on pieces of wool to form a design or to form the child's name.

Depending on the size of the heart envelope, it can be used to hold each child's Valentine cards or to carry home a few Valentine candies.

Heartlings

Butterflies, cats, birds, centipedes, mice, people, and rabbits can be made by gluing together hearts or half-hearts of various sizes.

Each child may want to make several Heartlings and hang them as a mobile, or a group of children may want to

display their Heartlings by stringing them from a wire coat hanger that has been bent into a heart shape and suspended from the ceiling.

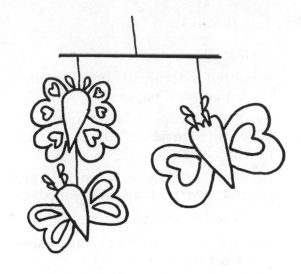

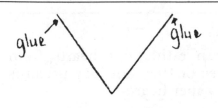

Add-a-Heart

A paper strip is folded in half and the two ends are brought up and glued with the outside edges together to form a heart.

Each consecutive strip is then brought through the last and glued to form a heart in the same manner.

Shiny Hearts

Many small hearts are cut from Valentine-colored tissue paper.

Larger hearts of varying sizes are cut from shiny-surfaced, white paper.

The tissue hearts are placed on the shiny hearts forming an overlapping mosaic, and are fixed with small amounts of glue.

When the shiny heart is completely covered, the surface is brushed with shellac and allowed to dry thoroughly.

The hearts can then be:

    scalloped

    mounted individually or in a grouping on colored paper

    used as a display background for Valentine stories or poems written by the children

    mounted individually on a larger colored heart with scalloped edges

    mounted on a large paper doily

    stapled back to back and suspended from the ceiling

Lacy Hearts

The children either cut hearts from paper doilies or they cut lacy patterns into plain, paper hearts.

These lacy hearts form stencils to be used in spatter or spray painting.

When painting, the children should be encouraged to use several stencils and to place them in a variety of ways.

For added effect, when the paint is dry reposition the stencils and spatter or spray the paper with a second color.

Crowns

Use four pieces of Valentine-colored construction paper to make this free-standing heart decoration.

Each piece of 8'' x 8'' (20 cm x 20 cm) paper is folded in half, and a heart and arrow shape is drawn on one.

The shaded areas are cut away and this figure is used as a pattern tracer on the three other pieces of paper.

These three figures are then cut out.

The four heart figures are stapled together at the top and at the tip of the arrow.

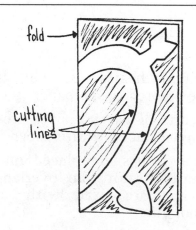

fold

cutting lines

The crown can then stand on desk tops or can be attached to the ends of crepe paper strips or brightly colored yarn.

On Valentine's Day, or at your Valentine's party, the children may wear their crowns. (Simply pull out the bottom sections on the hearts and the crown will fit the child's head.)

pull out here

DRAMATICS AND PHYSICAL ACTIVITIES

Friendship Chain

This singing game is most effectively played with a small group but it can be played with the entire class.

This game is played in the same way as ''Farmer in the Dell'' and the song is sung to the same tune.

A friendship chain we'll make,
A friendship chain we'll make,
Then round and round we'll turn about,
Clap hands and give a shout.

(Children stand in a circle.)

(They turn around individually.)
(They clap hands with a friend beside them.)

_____takes a friend,
_____takes a friend,
Skipping round the ring we go,
While_____takes a friend.

(The teacher chooses the first person to select a friend and skip around the inside of the circle clockwise holding hands, while children in the circle skip around individually counterclockwise.)

Now_____takes a friend,
Now_____takes a friend,
Skipping round the ring we go,
While_____takes a friend.

At the end of the chain, the children sing:

A friendship chain we've made,
A friendship chain we've made,
Round and round we turn about,
Clap hands and give a shout,
Hurray for friends!

113

Funny Valentines

The children pretend they are Funny Valentines by working in pairs. Once they are in pairs, they may do the following things:

> One child mimics the movements of the other.
>
> They may carry out tasks set by the teacher, using small equipment such as bean bags, hoops, skipping ropes, balls, and mats.
>
> They may use a combination of small equipment to create partner games.
>
> The children may wish to perform basic gynmastics which require a partner.
>
> They may create partner pantomimes through suggestions from the teacher.

WORKSHEETS

Page 116
Mend the Broken Hearts These hearts are cut out and the rhyming halves are matched and glued together on colored newsprint.

Page 117
Valen-twins The children draw lines to join the twins and then color the pairs identically. One heart does not have a mate.

Page 118
A Valentine The equations are completed and the Valentine is colored according to the code.

Pages 119, 120, 121
My Favorites Each child cuts out the heart-shaped pages and staples them together to form a booklet. He or she completes the sentence on each page and draws appropriate pictures.

Page 122
Heart Words The children decode the clues and print the words in the appropriate spaces on the crossword puzzle. Answers: Down 1. bow 2. card 4. eat 6. Cupid 7. name 8. you 9. heart 11. love 12. eye. Across 3. sweetheart 5. dart 6. candy 10. be mine 11. lace 13. Valentine's

Page 123
Numbers are friends, too! Arithmetic equations are printed in before duplicating.

Page 124
From My Heart Valentine letters are as much fun as Valentine cards. Letters to special friends may be written on this decorated paper and deposited in a Valentine mailbox. A hat and simple fabric mailbag could be created for the postal carrier.

Page 125

Valentines This entire worksheet can be given to each pupil, or the three Valentines can be cut apart and each child may choose one to complete according to the instructions given. The answers for the word puzzle are: Valentines, Arrow, Love, Envelope, Nice, Target, Ice cream, Nosegay, Eat Sweetheart.

Page 126

Jack of Hearts The children join the hearts alphabetically to complete the kite's tail.

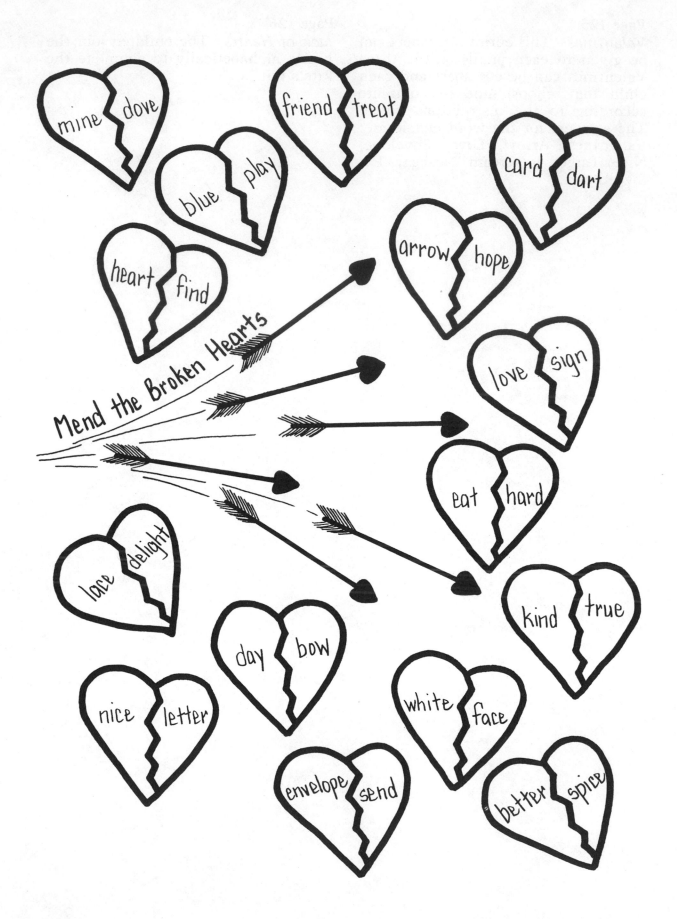

Mend the Broken Hearts

Valen-twins

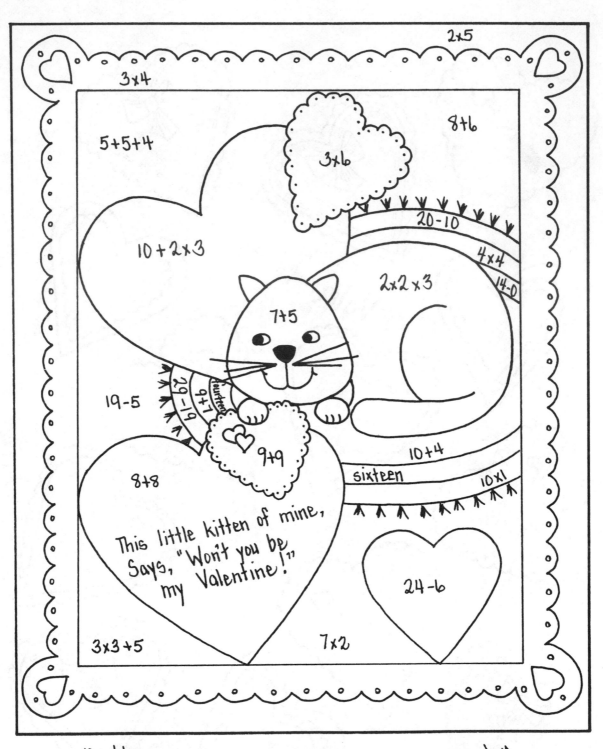

2×5

3×4

5+5+4

8+6

3×6

10+2×3

20-10

4×4

2×2×3

14-0

7+5

19-5

fourteen

7+6

9-14

9+9

10+4

8+8

sixteen

10×1

This little kitten of mine,
Says, "Won't you be
my Valentine!"

24-6

3×3+5

7×2

10 = blue
12 = yellow
14 = white
16 = red
18 = purple

A Valentine for you to color.
Complete the equations and color
according to the code.

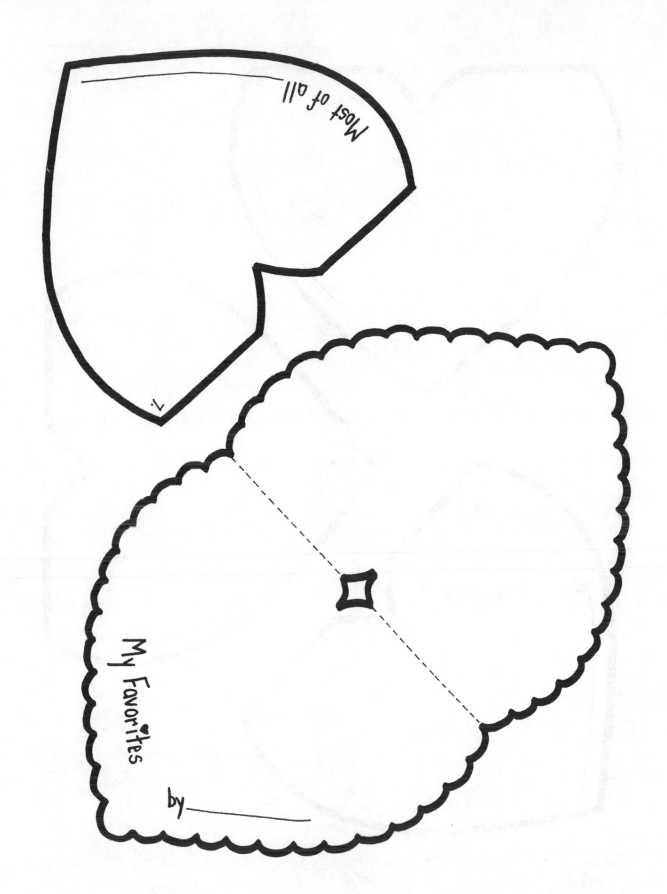

Most of all

My Favorites

by

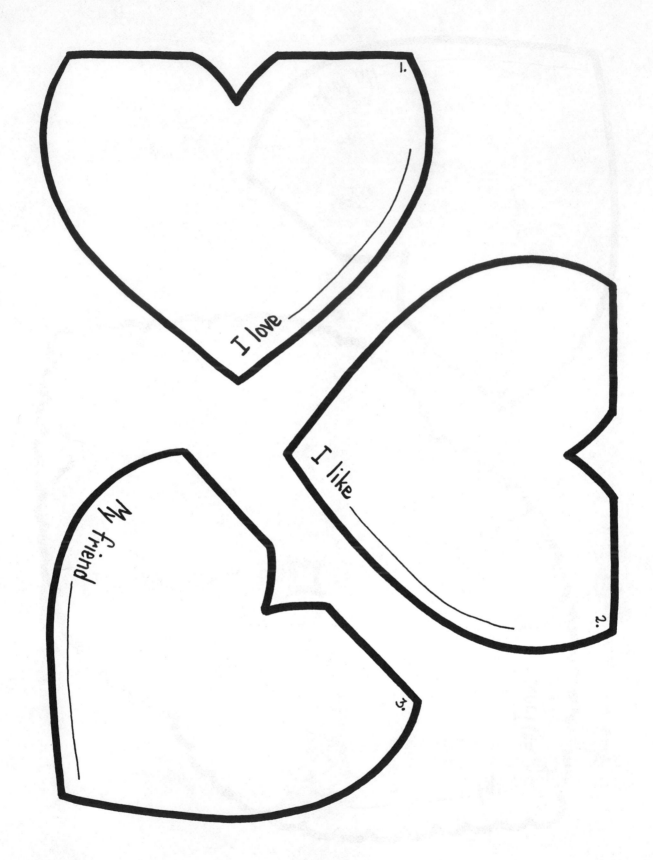

I love _____

I like _____

My friend _____

1.

2.

3.

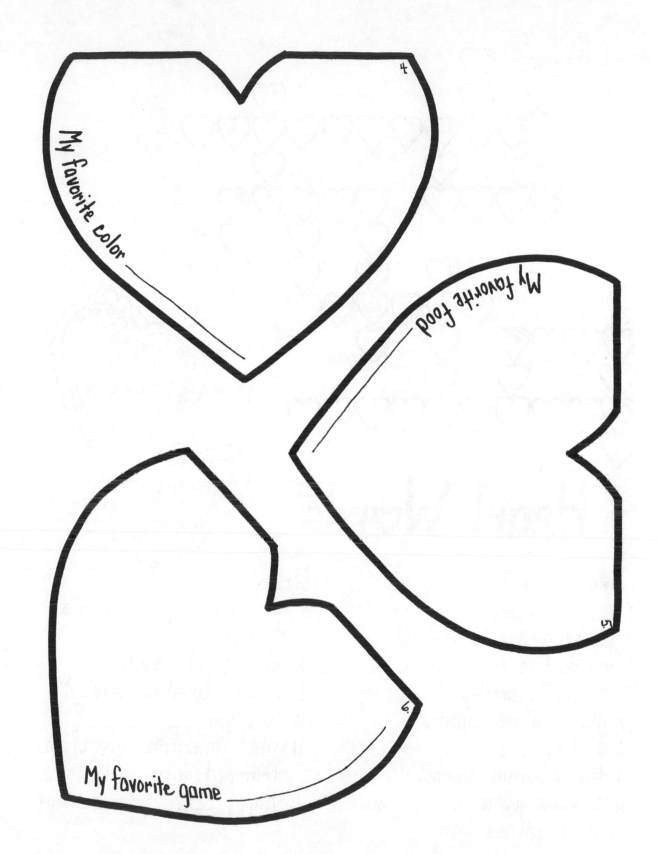

My favorite color _____

4.

My favorite food _____

5.

My favorite game _____

6.

Heart Words

Down:
1. ___ and arrow
2. you send this to a friend
4. you do this to 6 Across
6. he shoots arrows
7. what you are called
8. I love ___
9. the Valentine symbol
11. to know you is to ____ you
12. what you see with

Across:
3. what a man might call his girlfriend
5. what cupid sends
6. a nice Valentine present
10. Will you __ ____?
11. what Valentines are often trimmed with
13. Happy _____ Day!

From My Heart

VALENTINES
Cut these out and follow the instructions.

♥ Print or draw all the things that make you think of Valentine's Day!

♥ Scramble VALENTINES. Rearrange the letters and print as many new words as you can. You can use only those ten letters in the word.

V _ _ _ _ _ _ you send these to friends
A _ _ I _ _ you
L _ _ a card is inside this
E _ _ a friend is _ _ _ _ to have
N _ _ _ what Cupid shoots at
T _ _ a cold party treat
I _ _ _ a tiny bouquet of flowers
N _ _ _ _ _ Valentine cookies
E _ _ _ used with a bow
S _ _ you _ _ _ one you love

Display your finished work.

From *Special Things for Special Days* © 1980 by Goodyear Publishing Company, Inc.

Help Jack fly his kite. Draw the kite tail from ⓐ through to ⓩ.

BOOK LIST

Books for Valentine's Day

Bulla, Clyde Robert. *The Valentine Cat*. New York: Thomas Y. Crowell Co., 1959.

Cohen, Miriam. *Bee My Valentine*. New York: William Morrow and Co., 1976.

Haywood, Carolyn. *A Valentine Fantasy*. New York: William Morrow and Co., 1976.

Hopkins, Lee Bennett, ed. *Good Morning to You, Valentine*. New York: Harcourt, Brace, Jovanovich, 1976.

Krahn, Fernando. *Little Love Story*. New York: J. B. Lippincott, 1976.

de Paola, Tomie. *Things to Make and Do for Valentine's Day*. New York: Franklin Watts, 1976.

Schulz, Charles M. *Be My Valentine, Charlie Brown*. New York: Random House, 1976.

Schweninger, Ann. *The Hunt for Rabbit's Galosh*. New York: Doubleday, 1976.

Wahl, Jan. *Pleasant Fieldmouse's Valentine Trick*. New York: Windmill Books and E. P. Dutton, 1977.

Teacher's Resource Book

Barth, Edna. *Hearts, Cupids, and Red Roses: The Story of the Valentine Symbols*. New York: Seabury Press, 1974.

Books on Friendship

Fremlin, Robert. *Three Friends*. Toronto, Canada: Little Brown and Co., 1975.

Kafka, Sherry. *I Need a Friend*. New York: G. P. Putnam's Sons, 1971.

Norris, Gunilla B. *The Friendship Hedge*. New York: E. P. Dutton and Co., Inc. 1973.

Schulman, Janet. *The Big Hello*. New York: Greenwillow Books, 1976.

Sharmat, Marjorie Weinman. *I'm Not Oscar's Friend Anymore*. New York: E. P. Dutton and Co. Ltd., 1975.

Skorpen, Liesel Moak. *Plenty For Three*. New York: Coward, McCann, and Geoghegan, Inc., 1971.

Easter

WORKCARD SETS

Benjamin Bunny
Conversations

BOOKLETS

GAMES AND ACTIVITIES

Edible Necklaces
Egg-stra, Egg-stra
Sum Basket
Bunny Bonanza
Easy-Over
H.H. Hoppity
Scrambled Eggs
Things to Do with Eggs

HANDWORK

Egg Pictures
Scalloped Basket
Easter Bonnets
Egg Shell Scenes
Easter Parade
Easter Egg Tree
Recipe for Clay Dough
Bunnies
Woven Basket
Fingerpainted Eggs

DRAMATICS AND PHYSICAL ACTIVITIES

Movement
Pantomime
Drama
Easter Rabbit

WORKSHEETS

Whiskers
Dot-to-Dot
Tracing Trails
Eggs-act Match
A Bunny's Tale
Just Like a Bunny
The Egg Factory
Reginald Rabbit, Daffodil
    Duck, and Joe

BOOK LIST

Benjamin Bunny

Benjamin, a bunny with a pocketful of carrots, invites the children to choose one of his carrots and complete the task printed on it.

Many task cards should be made to accommodate individual abilities, or specific skills requiring practice.

Some examples of task cards are:

Go to the library and choose an Easter book to read.

Read a story to a friend.

Research and write five facts about rabbits.

Water the plants and tidy the counters.

Paint an Easter picture.

Measure the hallway in bunny hops.

Count the empty coat hooks.

Count and graph the types of eggs on the Easter Egg Tree.

Make an Easter card for a relative or friend.

Write a poem about the Easter Bunny.

Collect flowers to make a daisy-chain.

Choose and complete a jigsaw puzzle.

Scramble the letters of "Happy Easter" and write the new words.

Print five words that rhyme with "bunny".

List ten words that start with a short e as in "egg". Use each word in a sentence.

Put all these "bunny words" into alphabetical order: bunny, hopping fluffy, tail, floppy, ears, whiskers, twitching, nose, pink, white, furry, rabbit, hare, hole, carrot, cabbage, and lettuce.

How do you draw large rabbits or other characters when you have no artistic ability or interest? It's easy if you have an opaque projector. Simply place any outlined picture you want to copy in the opaque projector and reproduce it in the desired size on heavy paper. You, or a child, can trace the projected outline, adding color and details with paint, felt pens, or crayons. The completed character can be used to enhance displays, encourage desired work habits, attract attention to notices and reminders, denote centers, exhibit workcards, or stimulate story telling.

Conversations

A child chooses a card and creates the conversation that might be taking place between the animals on the card.

This may be done orally, with more than one child taking part in the conversation, or as an individual written exercise.

BOOKLETS

These individual or class-made booklets are more appealing to the students —and more attractive when completed —if they are in special shapes and have pastel-colored pages. These are some ideas for booklets:

Things that Can Hop

Things with Whiskers

Fluffy Things

Ways to Eat Eggs

Eggs are Laid by . . .

The Big Easter Egg Hunt

Easter Bonnets

Bunnies

GAMES AND ACTIVITIES

Edible Necklaces

Each child brings a small bag of candies to class. (The candies must be suitable for stringing.)

Using a tapestry needle and thread, the children string the candies they have chosen from the collected assortment.

These necklaces may be worn for the Easter party or the Easter Parade and can later be eaten.

When planning a party or special event where food will be served, have the children design placemats and placecards for themselves and their guests. They will enjoy decorating the craft paper or colored newsprint placemats with crayons and paper scraps, and writing appropriate slogans or messages on the placecards. Paper plates will no longer be a necessity, and serving and clean-up tasks will be made easier.

Egg-stra, Egg-stra

The children brainstorm and make a list of Easter words.

The teacher prints each of these words onto a colored paper Easter egg.

The children may wish do the following activities:

Arrange the eggs in alphabetical order.

Place the eggs in a chain fashion, making sure that each additional egg begins with the same letter as the last word ended with.

Sort the eggs into an egg carton that has been labeled with specific phonetic sounds.

Choose six words and use them in one sentence.

Choose one word and make a sentence containing words that begin with the letters in the chosen

word. For example: WHISKERS—
When Hopping Into Small Knolls
Easter Rabbit Stumbles. BUNNIES
—Bunnies Usually Nibble Nicely
If Eating Sweets.

Sum Basket

Two to four players take turns tossing ten numbered objects into a wicker basket.

After his or her turn the child must find the sum of the numbered objects in the basket.

The players awaiting their turns must make sure that the sums are correct.

Many objects can be labeled with numbers and used for tossing, including styrofoam eggs, erasers, bean bags, counting cubes, poker chips, sponge cubes, or large wooden beads.

The objects should be numbered to suit the ability levels of the children.

The playing time is set before the game begins.

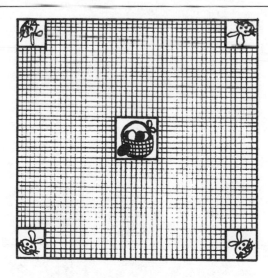

Bunny Bonanza

Two to four players participate.

Two dice are rolled and the total of the dice is added to give the player his or her move.

The players may move their markers forward, backward, and sideways, but not diagonally.

Small plastic bunnies would make ideal markers.

The winner is the first to arrive at the basket of eggs with an exact roll.

You can make a variety of dice using small wooden blocks. Using a felt-tipped marker, simply print on any numbers the children need practice with.

Easy-Over

This game is similar to Concentration, where the cards are scattered face down and two players alternate in turning the cards over to find the matching pairs.

The teacher can make the cards. Any of the following may be used in this game:

matching pairs of Easter eggs

number cards and corresponding picture cards

phonetic sound cards and corresponding picture cards

matching pairs of Easter symbols

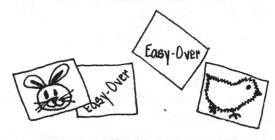

H. H. Hoppity

One child is chosen to be H. H. Hoppity.

He or she wears bunny ears attached to a headband and carries an Easter basket containing paper eggs on which the teacher has printed arithmetic equations.

The children stand or sit in a circle and H. H. Hoppity hops around in the middle and stands in front of one child.

The child facing H. H. Hoppity must pick one egg out of the Easter basket and answer the question that is printed on the egg.

If the child answers the equation correctly, he or she becomes H. H. Hoppity; if he or she does not answer correctly, H. H. Hoppity hops on to another child.

The equations on the eggs should be varied to suit the abilities of the children.

Scrambled Eggs

Scrambled Eggs can be made in many sizes, colors, and patterns. They may have a variety of messages printed on them.

The teacher can make several; older children may make them for younger children; or the children may make and exchange them with their classmates.

The number of strips the eggs are cut into depends on the difficulty desired.

Printed messages could include:

Hoppy Easter

Hopping down the bunny trail

A little bunny hopped by to say, Have a happy Easter Day.

Eggs of pink, yellow, and blue, Bring Easter happiness to you.

Things to Do with Eggs

Many things may be done with small chocolate eggs:

Weigh them.

Guess how many there are in various glass containers.

Discover how many there are per pound, etc.

Create arithmetic problems using them.

Balance other articles with them.

Have an Easter egg hunt.

Use them as rewards for special assignments well done.

Write stories pretending to be a chocolate egg that melts.

With candy-coated or sugar eggs of various sizes:

Sort them according to size and color.

Weigh them.

Compare their weights and sizes.

Use them, along with marshmallows and jellies, to make bunnies and chicks.

Write stories or poems about life as a candy egg.

With fresh eggs:

Compare the types, sizes, and costs of eggs available.

Cook and sample easy egg dishes.

Collect recipes for favorite egg dishes and compile them as an Easter gift for parents.

Have a resource person demonstrate the art of egg painting.

Hard-boil and decorate the eggs with crayons and paint.

With fertilized eggs:

Have a poultry farmer discuss his or her job.

Discover information on the life cycle of a chicken.

Compare and contrast animals that hatch from eggs.

Incubate fertilized eggs; record what happens daily.

Use what has been learned in movement, drama, writing, and speaking activities.

Have an Egg-fest to display and demonstrate what has been learned about eggs.

Serve some of those tasty egg "goodies".

HANDWORK

Egg Pictures

The children cut out construction paper eggs of various colors and sizes and use them to create Easter animals and scenes.

Crayoned details are added to complete the pictures.

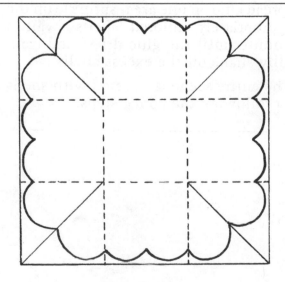

Scalloped Basket

The pattern shown makes a scalloped Easter basket.

Cut on the solid lines and fold on the dotted lines.

Overlap and glue the corner pieces that have diagonal cuts.

A handle and cut paper decorations can be added.

The completed baskets are used for collecting and sorting activities, or for holding Easter treats.

Easter Bonnets

Supply the children with such things as paper plates, crepe paper, ribbons, string, wool, tissue paper, egg cartons, paper cups, fabric scraps, pipe cleaners, colored construction paper, cellophane paper, or any other materials that are readily available.

The children choose the materials they desire and create a bonnet using the paper plate as a base.

Ties should be securely attached to the bonnets.

The finished bonnets may be worn at an Easter party or in an Easter parade.

If desired, a competition may be held in order to choose the funniest, prettiest, springiest, or most colorful bonnet.

Egg Shell Scenes

The children are instructed to bring clean, dry eggshells from home.

When enough of them have been collected, the eggshells are crushed with a rolling pin and tinted several shades with food coloring.

The children then draw uncluttered scenes and glue the eggshells on according to the desired color.

The children should be instructed to spread glue on one area; sprinkle on the appropriately colored shells; wait a minute until the glue dries; and carefully shake off the excess shells.

The entire scene is covered with shells by following the above steps.

Easter Parade

The beginnings of Easter characters are made when a child prints his or her hand by dipping it into thick paint and pressing it onto paper.

Other body parts are added using crayons or cut paper.

The completed and cut out Easter characters can form a parade along the walls.

Older children may enjoy printing the entire Easter character using various parts of their hand.

Here's another way to use those hand prints ~ make them into comic strip characters! Divide long narrow paper into sections by drawing lines or by folding and have the children place a hand or fingerprint in each section. They then use crayons or felt pens to develop their own comic strip character, background, other characters, and dialogue or story.

Begin with only three sections. This is easier for the children and also helps them to develop the idea that a story has a beginning, a middle, and an ending.

Easter Egg Tree

An Easter Egg Tree is made by sticking a bare branch or a few branches into a large pot containing rocks or plasticene.

If desired, the pot can be decorated, the branches can be sprayed a pastel color, or ribbons can be tied to the branches.

The following eggs can be hung with wool or ribbon from the branches.

CRAYON RESIST EGGS

Each child draws two egg shapes and decorates them by heavily coloring designs in bright colors.

Spaces must be left between the designs because a thin paint wash will be brushed over the surfaces of the eggs, providing the background color.

The eggs are then cut out, placed back to back, and stapled or glued together.

GLISTENING EGGS

The children draw and cut out egg shapes from colored construction paper.

The children paint designs on the eggs using thick paint and sprinkle the designs with salt while the paint is still wet. (Fine or coarse salt can be used.)

When each egg is dry, the design is repeated on its reverse side.

WAXED PAPER EGGS

Light-colored crayon shavings are placed between two layers of waxed paper.

These are then ironed, at a low setting, between sheets of newspaper. When cool, they can be cut into egg shapes.

These translucent eggs may be hung from the Easter Egg Tree as is, or with narrow, brightly colored paper frames.

CLAY DOUGH EGGS

A batch of clay dough may be divided into four parts and each part tinted a different color using food coloring.

A small lump of clay dough is flattened into an oval and is decorated by adding on bits of the different-colored dough.

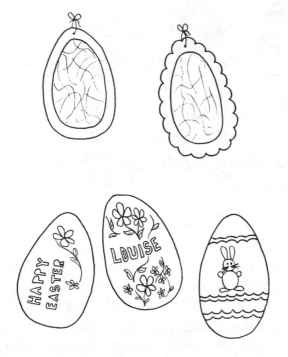

Recipe for Clay Dough

Mix 1 cup (227 ml) of flour and ½ cup (113.5 ml) of salt together in a bowl.

Slowly add water, squeezing with your hands until the mixture is a smooth, doughlike consistency.

142

Store the clay dough in a plastic bag or container with a lid.

Modelling is done on tin foil.

When the model is finished, bake it on the tin foil at 225°F (105° C). Small, thin models are baked about 15 minutes on each side. Larger, thicker objects can be baked up to one hour on each side.

The model may be colored by adding food coloring to the raw dough or by painting the model after baking.

Clear shellac may be used to protect the finish of the model after baking.

Small cookie cutters can be used in making clay dough decorations for the eggs.

Cookie cutters are available in a wide variety of shapes and sizes and can serve many purposes — tracing, printing designs, making cookies, creating Christmas tree ornaments, designing necklaces, and producing stick puppets.

Bunnies

TOILET ROLL BUNNY

Each child will need a toilet roll, a cottonball, and colored construction paper.

The toilet roll can be painted white or a pastel color, or it may be covered with a piece of construction paper.

The child then cuts paper eyes, ears, whiskers, feet, and a nose and glues them in place. The cottonball is used as a tail on the back of the bunny.

PAPER STRIP BUNNY

Paper strips of varying widths and lengths are used to make a bunny.

The teacher can have the strips precut for the children's use or each child can cut his or her own.

The children bend, fold, and glue the strips together to create their own bunnies.

CANDY BUNNIES

Each child will need two regular-sized marshmallows, two chocolate chips, and one miniature marshmallow; skinny black construction paper strips for whiskers; construction paper scraps for ears; and glue made by beating an egg white with icing sugar until it is thick and fluffy.

The marshmallows are glued forming the head and body; chocolate chips are glued on for eyes; black strip whiskers and construction paper ears are glued on; and the miniature marshmallow tail is attached.

If the bunnies are going to be taken home, they can be glued onto a plain or fancy piece of construction paper and wrapped with clear sandwich wrap.

FOLDED BUNNY

Fold a rectangular piece of colored construction paper in half lengthwise, outlining a bunny shape.

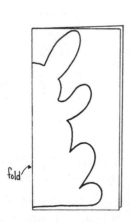

fold

Cut out the bunny, decorate it with scraps of colored paper, and glue on a cottonball tail.

After the bunny is completed, his front paws can be glued together to hold an Easter egg.

BUNNY FRIENDS

A rectangular piece of construction paper is folded into thirds.

On the top layer of the folded paper, an upright bunny is drawn so that his feet, front paws, and ears extend over the edges of the paper.

144

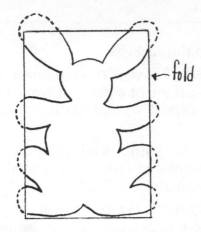

The bunny is cut out and unfolded, making a chain of three Bunny Friends.

Scraps can be used to decorate the bunnies.

The front paws of the two end bunnies may be glued together so the three bunnies are in a circle.

The bunnies can be grouped along shelves or in table displays, or they can be suspended from hoops, light fixtures, or ceilings.

Woven Basket

A piece of colored paper is folded in half and slits are cut into it from the fold, as shown in the illustration.

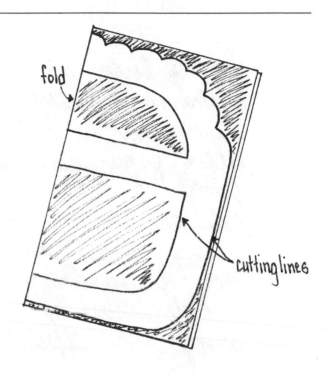

The paper is opened and different colored strips are woven in a variety of under-over patterns.

A second piece of colored paper (double the size of the first piece) is folded in half lengthwise and the center is cut away as shown.

This piece is then opened, forming a basket with a handle.

The basket section is placed over the woven paper and the two layers are stapled together.

145

Fingerpainted Eggs

Each child brushes thick paint over the entire surface of a piece of waxed paper and makes a design with his or her fingers.

When the paint is sticky, the child presses colored tissue-paper ovals over the entire area.

When completely dry, the paper can be cut into a large egg shape and mounted on a window that has a paper-grass border.

A grass border can be quickly and simply created on a paper cutter using green crepe paper or construction paper. Cut folded paper into desired widths and fringe deeply on the paper cutter; open out and attach to the window by placing rolled masking tape on the back of the fringed paper. Use several layers of paper grass for a bushy more effective result.

DRAMATICS AND PHYSICAL ACTIVITIES

Movement

Individual or class suggestions could include:

Hop like a bunny.

Waddle like a duckling.

Gambol like a lamb.

Prance like a colt.

Strut like a chick.

Glide like a cygnet.

Scamper like a puppy.

Creep like a kitten.
Flit like a butterfly.
Skitter like a baby bird.
Sway like a tulip.
Roll like an egg.

Pantomime

The class or a group could work to mime:

an Easter egg hunt

an Easter parade

delivering eggs

an Easter surprise

a Spring garden

a nest in Springtime

a farmyard in Spring

Drama

Characters to dramatize can be selected at random, or chosen and developed by the children.

Character suggestions for individual or group dramatization could include:

H. H. Hoppity	Grandpa Grey-Ears
Charles Chick	Beatrice Bunny
Daphne Duck	Miss Duckie
Rhonda Rabbit	Flutterby
Ted E. Bear	Chicklette
Kitty Cat	Chip Munk

Easter Rabbit

This is a circle game the children play as they sing the following song to the tune of "Yankee Doodle":

A furry Easter rabbit
Jumping up and down
Takes a friend and they hold hands
Hopping all a-round!

147

One child is chosen to stand inside the circle to be the first "Easter rabbit".

The "Easter rabbit" jumps up and down as the children sing the first two lines of the song.

When the children sing "takes a friend", the "Easter rabbit" chooses another child and they hold hands and hop around inside the circle.

The game continues with the children singing the song and each "Easter rabbit" choosing a friend.

When all the children have been chosen, they continue to hop around in a circle while they hum the tune three times.

WORKSHEETS

Page 150
Whiskers The children count the whiskers on the bunnies to discover the addition question. They then print the equation with the answer. For example, the first bunny has four whiskers on each side; thus $4 + 4 = 8$ would be printed. (A similar worksheet with the addends printed on the bunnies would also be valuable. The correct number of whiskers would be drawn in and the equation completed.)

Page 151
Dot-to-Dot The letters of the alphabet are joined to find this Easter character.

Page 152
Tracing Trails The trails of these characters are traced in crayon across the page.

Page 153
Eggs-act Match Color words, rhyming words, synonyms, antonyms, sight words, or arithmetic equations and their answers are printed on the egg halves before duplicating. The eggs on the page are then cut out, and the correct halves matched and glued onto a sheet of colored newsprint.

Coloring and activity books are fine sources of dot-to-dots, mazes, and puzzles in many themes.

Page 154

A Bunny's Tale This page is duplicated on lined or colored paper. The children could write a story about a bunny, or a story that a rabbit might tell. When the stories are finished, the bunnies are cut out and displayed along a woodland trail or in a parade.

Page 155

Just Like a Bunny The child draws, and identifies by labeling, other living things that have ears, whiskers, and tails.

Page 156

The Egg Factory This is a sheet for creative thinking. You may encourage the children to draw and then record their ideas in printing or on a tape recorder. They may describe what the factory looks like; who the employer is; who the workers are and what roles they play in the egg production; what varieties of eggs are produced; what the market is; and how they are packaged and marketed.

Pages 157, 158, 159

Reginald Rabbit, Daffodil Duck, and Joe These three characters can be used for stick puppets, paper bag puppets, or worn as masks. They are used to promote creative thinking and speaking. One two, or all of the characters can be used at a time. Perhaps the teacher may wish to supply situations or predicaments for the characters to deal with.

Whiskers

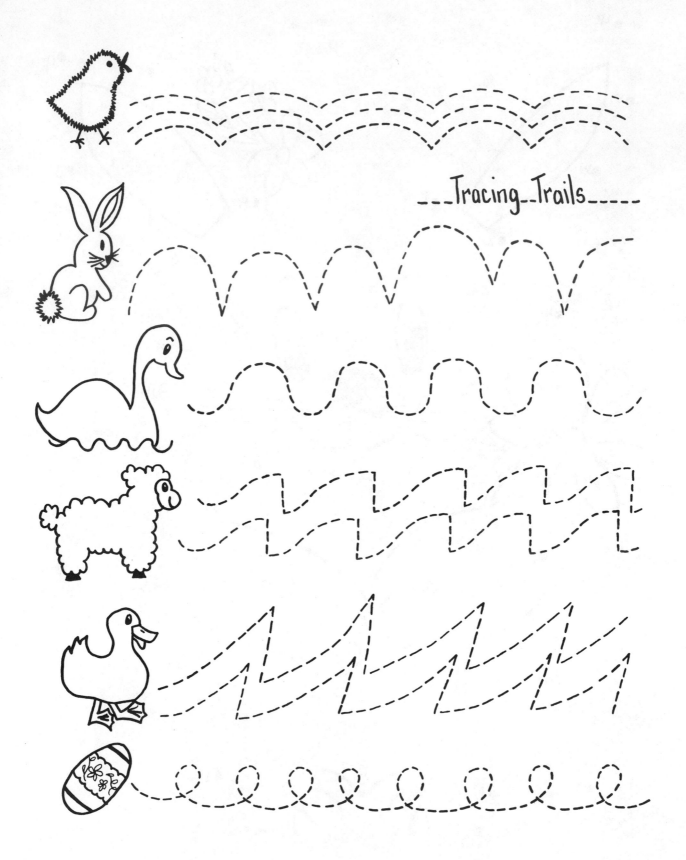

Tracing Trails

From *Special Things for Special Days* © 1980 by Goodyear Publishing Company, Inc.

Eggs-act Match

A
Bunny's Tale
by ———

154

Just Like a Bunny...

The Egg Factory

158

BOOKLIST

Adams, Adrienne. *The Easter Egg Artists*. New York: Charles Scribner's Sons, 1976.

Balian, Lorna. *Humbug Rabbit*. New York: Abingdon Press, 1974.

Heyward, Du Bose. *The Country Bunny and the Little Gold Shoes*. Boston: Houghton Mifflin, 1939.

Marianna. *Miss Flora McFlimsey's Easter Bonnet*. New York: Lothrop, Lee, and Shepard Co., 1951.

Tresselt, Alvin. *The World in the Candy Egg*. New York: Lothrop, Lee, and Shepard Co., 1967.

Weil, Lisl. *The Candy Egg Bunny*. New York: Holiday House, 1975.

Wiersum, Beverly Rae. *The Story of Easter for Children*. Milwaukee, Wisconsin: Ideals, 1979.

Young, Miriam. *Miss Suzy's Easter Surprise*. New York: Parents' Magazine Press, 1972.

Teacher's Resource Book:

Barth, Edna. *Lilies, Rabbits, and Painted Eggs: The Story of the Easter Symbols*. New York: Seabury Press, 1970.